The Developing Child
Student Workbook

Glencoe
McGraw-Hill

New York, New York   Columbus, Ohio   Woodland Hills, California   Peoria, Illinois

Glencoe/McGraw-Hill

A Division of The McGraw·Hill Companies

Printed in the United States of America

Send all inquiries to:
Glencoe/McGraw-Hill
3008 West Willow Knolls Drive
Peoria, Illinois 61614-1083

ISBN 0-02-642711-7 Student Workbook

9 10 024 04

CONTENTS

Chapter 7: The Baby's Arrival

Chapter 8: Physical Development During the First Year

Chapter 9: Emotional and Social Development During the First Year

Chapter 10: Intellectual Development During the First Year

Chapter 11: Physical Development from One to Three

Chapter 12: Emotional and Social Development from One to Three

Chapter 13: Intellectual Development from One to Three

Learning About Children

Study Guide

Directions. As you read the chapter, answer the following questions. Later, you can use this guide to study the information in the chapter.

Section 1-1: Beginning Your Study of Children

1. In what two ways are the connections between nerve cells formed in children's brains? _____

_____

_____

2. In what five ways do children benefit from play? _____

_____

_____

3. How can you benefit from studying children? _____

_____

_____

_____

_____

4. Why would it help a caregiver to understand the behaviors that are appropriate for a child of a certain age?

_____

_____

Section 1-2: Understanding Childhood

5. In what sense is childhood a recent discovery, even though there have always been children?

_____

_____

_____

(Continued on next page)

6. Give examples of the differences between childhood in the past and today.

_____

_____

_____

7. Briefly describe the findings of each of the following theorists of child development.

A. Freud _____

B. Montessori _____

C. Piaget _____

D. Coles _____

8. What do the pathways in the brain do? _____

_____

_____

9. Identify approximately when the brain begins to control the following functions:

A. Motor development _____

B. Vision _____

C. Vocabulary _____

10. Explain in your own words what the following characteristics of development mean.

A. Development is similar for everyone. _____

_____

_____

B. Development builds on earlier learning. _____

_____

_____

C. Development proceeds at an individual rate. _____

_____

_____

D. The different areas of development are interrelated. _____

_____

_____

(Continued on next page)

Learning About Children   *Chapter 1 continued*

    E. Development is continuous throughout life. _____

_____

_____

11. Name two major influences on development and give an example of each. _____

_____

_____

12. What are three developmental tasks of adolescence? _____

_____

_____

_____

13. What are the developmental tasks of different stages of adulthood, and when do they typically take place?

_____

_____

_____

_____

_____

Section 1-3: Observing Young Children

14. What are the benefits of observing children? _____

_____

_____

_____

_____

15. Which is the most useful way of writing observations? Why? _____

_____

_____

_____

(Continued on next page)

16. Describe each type of observation record, and explain when to use it.

A. Running record _____

_____

_____

_____

B. Anecdotal record _____

_____

_____

_____

C. Frequency count _____

_____

_____

_____

D. Developmental checklist _____

_____

_____

_____

17. Where should you position yourself and how should you act when observing? _____

_____

_____

_____

18. Explain confidentiality in connection with observation records. _____

_____

_____

_____

_____

(Continued on next page)

Learning About Children   *Chapter 1 continued*

Section 1-4: Working with Children

19. Name three levels of jobs and give examples of each. _____

_____

_____

_____

20. How can you learn about careers? _____

_____

_____

_____

21. What factors can you use to evaluate a career? _____

_____

_____

_____

_____

22. What skills will you need in the future to succeed in a career? _____

_____

_____

_____

_____

_____

THE DEVELOPING CHILD: **Student Workbook**

Beginning Your Study of Children    **SECTION 1-1**

Thinking About Children

Directions. Complete the following sentences with the first thoughts that enter your mind. There are no right or wrong answers.

1. Studying about children can help me … _____

_____

2. What I like most about children is … _____

_____

3. What I like least about children is … _____

_____

4. As a child, I was … _____

_____

5. My favorite activity as a child was … _____

_____

6. The thing I remember most about my childhood is … _____

_____

7. Children need parents to care for them because … _____

_____

8. As a parent, I would like to be … _____

_____

9. Most of my knowledge of children has come from … _____

_____

10. All children all alike in that they … _____

_____

11. All children are different in that they … _____

_____

(Continued on next page)

Beginning Your Study of Children   *Section 1-1 continued*

12. The hardest thing for a child to learn is … _____

_____

13. One thing I learned as a child and never forgot is … _____

_____

14. I don't understand why children … _____

_____

15. To me, a newborn baby is … _____

_____

16. My favorite age for a child is … _____

_____

17. When I am with children, I … _____

_____

18. One thing I hope to learn in this class is … _____

_____

Understanding Childhood

Describing Development

Directions. Identify the characteristic of development described in each situation. Choose one of the characteristics listed in the box below and write it in the answer space.

CHARACTERISTICS OF DEVELOPMENT

Development is similar for everyone.
Development builds on earlier learning.
Development proceeds at an individual rate.
The different areas of development are interrelated.
Development continues throughout life.

---

1. Inez lives in a home with her parents, a brother and sister, and her grandparents. Her grandparents are now retired from working. They help watch the younger children while Inez's parents are at work.

_____

_____

2. In school, Michael did poorly on tests and was seldom able to answer the teacher's questions. Other children teased him and called him names. As a result, he was shy and had little self-confidence. Since he has started wearing glasses, he has been seeing the chalkboard better and doing better in school. He feels better about himself and is now getting along better with the other children.

_____

_____

3. Josh and Nicole are cousins. Although Josh is two months older, Nicole began to sit and stand at about the same time he did.

_____

_____

4. Dante was looking at the pictures in the family photo album. He saw photos of his daughter Becky when she was an infant and started lifting herself on her arms and legs. About a month later, she began crawling, and then stood up while holding on to furniture. Now Becky moves about the room by "cruising"— walking while touching furniture.

_____

_____

(Continued on next page)

Understanding Childhood   *Section 1-2 continued*

5. Dana and her family spent the summer visiting relatives in Toronto. Dana helped the parents by watching Michelle and Brian, who were both two years old. She noticed that both children could run fairly well, stand on one foot, and climb stairs. They both enjoyed playing with sand and liked finger painting.

_____

_____

6. Terry, Rachel, and Juan all attend the same child care center. Terry is slightly shorter than the other two. She enjoys being with others and plays well with others. Rachel is the tallest and most coordinated. She tends to stay near the center's workers and spends little time with the children. Juan is of average size. He plays quietly by himself although he joins in group activities when they are scheduled.

_____

_____

7. Jessica is an active three-year-old. Lately, she has started choosing her clothes each morning. Her parents are amazed at her eagerness to learn new things—it seems she never stops wanting to learn.

_____

_____

8. Luke is helping his younger brother Andy learn the alphabet. Andy seems to be catching on very quickly. Yesterday, he called out some of the letters on a store sign as he and Luke walked down the street. Luke knows that soon Andy will be able to point out a few simple words and not long after that he'll be reading sentences.

_____

_____

Observing Young Children

Developing Observation Skills

Directions. The information below is part of an observation record. Read it and then answer the questions that follow.

About the Observation

Child: Girl named Jacki   **Age:** 14 months

Setting: Jacki's home with her father and four-year-old brother; during the observation, her mother came home

Time: 4:00 P.M.–5:00 P.M

Purpose: To examine her development in all areas.

Notes

Jacki sits on floor playing with interlocking blocks while brother builds a garage with others … takes some blocks out of box and puts them back … puts a small block in her mouth … father tells her to take it out … she looks at him and does nothing … father starts to walk toward her … she takes block out of her mouth and throws it on the floor … stands up, using her hand to push against floor … has no trouble getting to her feet … walks to her brother … picks up some of blocks near him … he tells her to put them down … she tries to run away … her steps are quick, not quite a run … her legs are somewhat stiff … brother follows her … she climbs on couch and bangs blocks together … father says, "Jacki, would you like a book?" … she drops blocks on floor … brother takes blocks away and returns to building … Jacki turns around and slides down off couch … walks to get picture book about little bear … father sits on couch … she walks back to couch saying "Beah, Beah" … climbs onto couch while still holding book … gives book to father and sits in his lap … smiles as father begins to read

---

1. What type of observation record is this? _____

2. Write your interpretation of the observation in each of the following areas:

A. Social development _____

B. Intellectual development _____

C. Physical development _____

D. Emotional development _____

E. Moral development _____

F. Possible problems and concerns _____

Working with Children

Occupational Interests

Directions. Read the following statements. Place a check (✔) in the column that best describes your opinion. There are no right or wrong answers. Then answer the questions that follow.

Statement	Agree	Disagree	Unsure
1. I like children.	_____	_____	_____
2. I am patient.	_____	_____	_____
3. I like to work with my hands.	_____	_____	_____
4. I enjoy helping people learn.	_____	_____	_____
5. I am creative.	_____	_____	_____
6. I am even-tempered.	_____	_____	_____
7. I am enthusiastic.	_____	_____	_____
8. I like to work independently.	_____	_____	_____
9. I am responsible.	_____	_____	_____
10. I have a sense of humor.	_____	_____	_____
11. I am flexible.	_____	_____	_____
12. I love being around people.	_____	_____	_____
13. I make sound judgments.	_____	_____	_____
14. I can handle an emergency.	_____	_____	_____
15. I understand children's needs.	_____	_____	_____
16. I understand stages of development.	_____	_____	_____
17. I am sensitive to others' feelings.	_____	_____	_____
18. I am able to communicate effectively.	_____	_____	_____
19. I enjoy entertaining children.	_____	_____	_____
20. I like to help others solve their problems.	_____	_____	_____

(Continued on next page)

THE DEVELOPING CHILD: Student Workbook   **17**

Statement	Agree	Disagree	Unsure
21. I am considerate of others.	_____	_____	_____
22. I have lots of energy.	_____	_____	_____
23. I am a good listener.	_____	_____	_____
24. I am dependable.	_____	_____	_____
25. I like to serve the public.	_____	_____	_____
26. I enjoy organizing activities.	_____	_____	_____
27. I get along with all kinds of people.	_____	_____	_____
28. I enjoy learning new ideas and skills.	_____	_____	_____
29. I can explain things clearly.	_____	_____	_____
30. I am honest and truthful with others.	_____	_____	_____

31. Rank the following values related to career satisfaction in order of their importance to you. Number the items from 1 to 9 in the space provided, with 1 being the most important.

_____ money   _____ fame   _____ security

_____ variety   _____ service to others   _____ challenge

_____ power   _____ self-expression   _____ independence

32. What do your answers tell you about your strengths? _____

_____

33. What do your answers tell you about your values? _____

_____

Learning About Families

CHAPTER 2

Study Guide

Directions. As you read the chapter, answer the following questions. Later, you can use this guide to study the information in the chapter.

Section 2-1: Understanding Families

1. What are two functions families perform? _____

_____

_____

_____

2. What are some of the ways in which families meet the needs of children? _____

_____

_____

_____

3. How do families pass on values? _____

_____

_____

4. Give an example of each of the following types of families.

   A. Nuclear _____

   B. Single-parent _____

   C. Blended _____

   D. Extended _____

5. Name and describe three ways of becoming a parent other than by being a biological parent.

_____

_____

_____

_____

(Continued on next page)

6. Describe the following stages of the family life cycle.

    A. Launching _____

    B. Middle age _____

    C. Beginning _____

    D. Developing _____

    E. Retirement _____

    F. Expanding _____

7. Read the following account of one family. Then in the lines that follow, indicate what trends are affecting this family. Describe what consequences each trend might have on their lives.

> Jack and Amber Henderson just moved from the west coast to the east. All the rest of their family still lives in the West except for Jack's mother, who has come to live with them. The family moved because Jack's company had transferred him. The transfer came with a promotion and a raise, which will be helpful because Amber is pregnant with their third child. She works at home, using a computer and a fax machine to communicate with her customers.

_____

_____

_____

_____

_____

_____

_____

_____

8. Give an example of how scheduling and organization can help families control stress. Give one example for each.

_____

_____

_____

_____

(Continued on next page)

Section 2-2: What Parenthood Means

9. Give an example of one of the changes that parenthood brings. _____

_____

_____

10. What do you think is the most important reward of parenthood? Why? _____

_____

_____

11. Explain in your own words why each of the following considerations is important to the decision of whether to have children.

A. Emotional maturity _____

B. Desire for parenthood _____

C. Health _____

D. Management skills _____

E. Financial considerations _____

Understanding Families

Identifying Characteristics of Families

Directions. Read each of the examples and answer the questions that follow.

Kyle and Meredith

Kyle and Meredith are married. Meredith has found a job in the field that she prepared for, but Kyle found that the industry he trained for is in an economic downturn, and none of the companies are hiring. While he waits for that situation to change, he is caring for their child, who is a year old.

---

1. What kind of family structure are they? _____

2. What stage of the family life cycle are they in? _____

3. What trend is affecting this family? _____

Karl and Aleeta

Karl had two children from his first marriage. His first wife died, and two years later he married Aleeta, who had been single. The children are now in college. Aleeta is younger than Karl and wants to have children of her own. Karl is not sure that he's ready to take the responsibility of raising a child all over again. He's also worried that one of his aged parents may die and he and Aleeta may have to take the other into their home.

---

4. What type of family structure is this? _____

5. What stage of the family life cycle are they in? _____

6. What trend is affecting this family? _____

(Continued on next page)

Understanding Families   *Section 2-1 continued*

Jean-Louis and Clothilde

Jean-Louis and Clothilde have recently moved to the United States to make a better life for themselves and their children. Jean-Louis is studying computers so he can get a secure job. Like many immigrants, they are starting out by living with relatives who came here earlier. Their son and daughter are in junior high school.

---

7. What kind of family structure are they? _____

8. What stage of the family life cycle are they in? _____

9. What trend is affecting this family? _____

Florence and Becky

Florence's husband left her two years earlier, and she and her daughter have struggled ever since. Florence works while Becky is in school and takes classes at night so she can improve her job skills and earn more money. She also works weekends, when she leaves Becky in the care of her parents

---

10. What kind of family structure are they? _____

11. What stage of the family life cycle are they in? _____

12. What trend is affecting this family? _____

What Parenthood Means

Management Skills

Directions. Management skills involve five steps. Read each of the situations described below. In the middle column, indicate which step it involves. In the right column, indicate whether you think the person described is acting wisely and explain your reasoning. After analyzing these situations, answer question 8 on the next page.

STEPS IN MANAGEMENT SKILLS

Setting goals
Identifying resources
Making a plan
Putting the plan in action
Reevaluating the plan

Situation	Step Involved	Your Evaluation
1. Marlene used a computer program to prepare a budget to manage her family's expenses.		
2. Laurence faced a problem at work. He tried to think of what person he knew could give him advice about this problem.		
3. Vikki wanted to exercise to lose weight.		

(Continued on next page)

What Parenthood Means   *Section 2-2 continued*

Situation	Step Involved	Your Evaluation
4. Carole bought a dress without trying it on. After bringing it home, she found out it didn't fit. Talking to a friend about it, she said, "I guess I won't do that again. Do you want to go shopping?"		
5. Reynaldo wanted to learn how to play the piano. He practiced once every two weeks.		
6. Mei Ling was looking for a job. She spent 15 minutes every day looking quickly through the want ads in the newspaper.		
7. Kidlyn made a chart to keep track of how she used her time each week. She highlighted the blocks of time that she had free.		

8. Describe how you can use these steps to improve how you manage. _____

_____

_____

_____

_____

THE DEVELOPING CHILD: Student Workbook

Effective Parenting Skills

CHAPTER 3

Study Guide

Directions. As you read the chapter, answer the following questions. Later, you can use this guide to study the information in the chapter.

Section 3-1: What Is Parenting?

1. Give a brief definition of parenting. _____

_____

_____

2. How can having reasonable expectations of children help a parent use good judgment?

_____

_____

_____

_____

3. Give an example of each type of parenting style.

A. Authoritarian style _____

B. Democratic style _____

C. Permissive style _____

4. In what five ways can parents develop parenting skills? _____

_____

_____

_____

_____

5. How are children affected by nurturing? How are they affected by deprivation? _____

_____

_____

_____

_____

(Continued on next page)

6. Name three techniques for good communication. _____

_____

_____

_____

_____

_____

Section 3-2: Guiding Children's Behavior

7. Give three outcomes of effective guidance. _____

_____

_____

_____

8. Why is consistency important when dealing with children? _____

_____

_____

_____

9. What are the three keys to effective guidance? _____

_____

_____

_____

10. Give an example of positive reinforcement at work. _____

_____

_____

11. Marisa's mother said to her "I'm so proud of you when you dress yourself." Was this effective praise? If not, how would you reword it?

_____

_____

_____

(Continued on next page)

12. Why do children respond well to being offered choices? _____

_____

_____

13. What three questions should parents consider in setting limits? _____

_____

_____

_____

_____

14. A father told his daughter, "You can't go outside after dark." Is that an effective limit? Why or why not?

_____

_____

15. What three questions should a caregiver ask before responding to a child's misbehavior?

_____

_____

_____

_____

_____

_____

16. Give an example of intentional misbehavior and unintentional misbehavior. _____

_____

_____

17. List three positive types of negative reinforcement. _____

_____

_____

18. Choose one of the poor disciplinary methods and explain why it is not effective.

_____

_____

_____

(Continued on next page)

Section 3-3: Child Care Options

19. What social trends are increasing the demand for child care? _____

_____

_____

_____

_____

20. Who do you think would benefit most from care in the child's own home, a child of nine months or a child of five years? Why?

_____

_____

_____

21. Why is the illness of the caregiver more of a problem with family child care than with center-based care?

_____

_____

_____

22. What are the advantages and disadvantages of play groups?_____

_____

_____

_____

23. What is the value of accreditation? _____

_____

_____

24. What does Head Start offer in addition to educational activities? _____

_____

_____

25. What are the ages of children who attend preschools? _____

_____

_____

(Continued on next page)

26. What factors do parents consider in evaluating child care? _____

_____

_____

_____

27. Where can people find information on child care available? _____

_____

_____

_____

28. Why should parents visit a center before choosing it? Why visit after a child has already been placed in the center?

_____

_____

_____

_____

What Is Parenting?

Parenting and You

Directions. The satisfaction someone receives from being a parent may depend on how the child meets the parents' expectations. If you were a parent, what expectations would you have for your child? Read each trait listed below. Place a check (✔) in the column that best describes your opinion of the importance of that trait for your child. Then answer the questions that follow.

Statement	Very Important	Somewhat Important	Not Important
1. Achieves good grades in school.	_____	_____	_____
2. Be neat and clean.	_____	_____	_____
3. Excel in sports.	_____	_____	_____
4. Be independent.	_____	_____	_____
5. Be a leader.	_____	_____	_____
6. Have good manners.	_____	_____	_____
7. Be obedient.	_____	_____	_____
8. Respect authority.	_____	_____	_____
9. Have a sense of humor.	_____	_____	_____
10. Be creative.	_____	_____	_____
11. Be adventuresome.	_____	_____	_____
12. Have self-confidence.	_____	_____	_____
13. Be assertive.	_____	_____	_____
14. Be physically attractive.	_____	_____	_____
15. Be popular with peers.	_____	_____	_____
16. Be loyal to friends.	_____	_____	_____
17. Be honest.	_____	_____	_____
18. Have strong religious beliefs or principles.	_____	_____	_____
19. Be responsible.	_____	_____	_____
20. Be generous and helpful to others.	_____	_____	_____

(Continued on next page)

21. Identify the five traits you feel are most important to a child. You may choose them from the list on pages 33-34 or add others you feel are important. Write them in order on the lines below, starting with the most important.

_____

_____

_____

_____

22. Does your list of most important traits depend on whether the child is a boy or girl? Explain.

_____

_____

_____

23. As a parent, what would you do to help your child develop the five traits you have listed?

_____

_____

_____

_____

Guiding Children's Behavior

Being Positive

Directions. Children are more likely to behave well when you give guidance using positive language. Read the following statements. Then rewrite each so that it is more positive.

1. Don't throw the ball! _____

_____

2. Keep your hands off the glass vase! _____

_____

3. Don't spill your milk! _____

_____

4. How many times have I told you not to leave toys on the floor? _____

_____

5. Stop pulling the cat's tail! _____

_____

6. Don't drop your toy in the water! _____

_____

7. Don't eat cookies before dinner! _____

_____

8. Stop yanking on your sister's hair! _____

_____

9. Don't forget to pick up your books! _____

_____

10. Don't hit the table with your wooden hammer! _____

_____

(Continued on next page)

Directions. Caregivers who explain reasons get better results than those who only use sharp commands. Listed below are a number of daily activities. Write what you would say to persuade a resisting child to do each. Be as positive and helpful as possible.

11. Get ready for bed. _____

_____

12. Eat your dinner now. _____

_____

13. Pick up toys. _____

_____

14. Get dressed. _____

_____

15. Do something well. _____

_____

16. Get hands and face washed. _____

_____

17. Brush teeth. _____

_____

18. Play quietly. _____

_____

Child Care Options

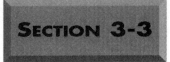

Evaluating Child Care Choices

Directions. Read the following statements about child care. Then rank them in order of their importance to you by writing a number from 1 to 10 in the space provided. When you're done ranking them, complete the rest of the worksheet.

_____ **A.** Caregivers are licensed or the center is accredited.

_____ **B.** The ratio of child care workers to children meets NAEYC standards.

_____ **C.** The setting is a home.

_____ **D.** The setting is a child care center.

_____ **E.** Children have the opportunity for free play; the entire day is not structured.

_____ **F.** There are a variety of materials for children to play with.

_____ **G.** Caregivers provide parents with monthly reports.

_____ **H.** Caregivers allow parents to visit anytime they want.

_____ **I.** The caregiver has flexible hours.

_____ **J.** The caregiver also is caring for her own child.

Now choose the items that you ranked 1 through 3. In the lines that follow, explain why they are the most important to you.

_____

_____

_____

_____

_____

_____

_____

_____

Teen Pregnancy and Parenthood

CHAPTER 4

Study Guide

Directions. As you read the chapter, answer the following questions. Later, you can use this guide to study the information in the chapter.

Section 4-1: The Realities of Teen Pregnancy

1. What is the difference between sexuality and sexual activity? _____

_____

_____

_____

2. Explain each of the following aspects of sexuality.

A. Physical _____

_____

B. Emotional _____

_____

C. Social _____

_____

3. What values might a teen use to help make difficult decisions? Pick one of the values that you named and explain how it could help you to make the right decision.

_____

_____

_____

4. What is a sexually transmitted disease? _____

_____

5. What is the only guaranteed way to prevent STDs? _____

_____

6. Besides STDs, what is a possible consequence of sexual activity? _____

_____

(Continued on next page)

Teen Pregnancy and Parenthood   *Chapter 4 continued*

7. What are the four types of problems created by teen pregnancy? _____

_____

_____

_____

8. What medical problems are teen mothers more likely to face than any other group?

_____

_____

_____

9. How can money problems affect teen couples? _____

_____

_____

_____

10. In what ways can pregnancy cause stress? _____

_____

_____

_____

Section 4-2: Solving Problems

11. What are the parts of the problem-solving process? _____

_____

_____

_____

_____

12. What two things should you remember when identifying consequences? _____

_____

_____

_____

_____

(Continued on next page)

THE DEVELOPING CHILD: Student Workbook   **37**

13. What are some reasons to abstain from sexual activity? _____

_____

_____

_____

14. What is the first thing a teen should do when she believes she is pregnant? _____

_____

_____

15. What special challenges does a single parent face?_____

_____

_____

16. What are some of the advantages and disadvantages of pregnant teens choosing to marry?

_____

_____

_____

_____

_____

17. Explain the two types of adoption. _____

_____

_____

_____

The Realities of Teen Pregnancy

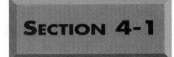

SECTION 4-1

Pledging Abstinence

Directions. Many students recognize that abstinence is the only certain way to avoid the problems associated with sexual activity—whether those problems are pregnancy or sexually transmitted diseases. Across the country, many students are writing and signing abstinence pledges, in which they promise to avoid sexual activity. Students committed to this choice sign the pledge and then make sure that they live according to their promises.

Using the spaces below, write your own version of an abstinence pledge. Think about these questions before you write:

- What would you say in the pledge?
- How general should it be?
- Should males and females who are dating each other both sign such a pledge? If so, would the language of the pledge be different?
- What role should parents play in the pledge?

_____

_____

_____

_____

_____

_____

_____

_____

_____

_____

_____

_____

_____

_____

_____

_____

_____

_____

Solving Problems

Applying the Problem-Solving Process

Directions. Read the following situation and help Mary come to a decision by going through each stage of the problem solving process.

> Caitlin, who is Mary's best friend, has been dating Greg for over a year. One weekend, Caitlin was out of town with her family—they were visiting relatives in another state. That Saturday night, Mary went to the movies with a group of friends, and while they were there she saw Greg with another girl. She knows that Caitlin cares a lot for Greg, and she's afraid that the news will hurt her friend. On the other hand, she's angry that her friend's trust is being abused.

1. What problem does Mary face? _____

_____

2. List all the information you have about Mary's problem. _____

_____

_____

3. What are three possible alternatives for Mary? _____

_____

_____

4. For each alternative, what are some possible consequences? _____

_____

_____

_____

_____

_____

_____

_____

_____

(Continued on next page)

Solving Problems   *Section 4-2 continued*

5. Of the alternatives you listed, which one do you think is the best? Why? _____

_____

_____

_____

_____

6. Would the alternative you chose require any type of plan in order to be carried out? If so, explain the plan.

_____

_____

_____

_____

7. Mary decided to tell Caitlin; she felt that was the most loyal thing she could do for her friend. Very upset, Caitlin called Greg. At first Greg denied taking the girl to the movie. Later, he admitted it and said there was nothing wrong with what he did. Caitlin broke up with him. Do you think Mary was right in solving the problem as she did? Why or why not?

_____

_____

_____

_____

8. Suppose Mary decided to tell Caitlin, but the outcome was different. Suppose that Caitlin was very upset for several days. Finally, she talked to Greg, who told her that the girl was the daughter of some friends of his parents; the friends had been visiting for the weekend, and suggested that he and the daughter see a movie. Do you think Mary was right in solving the problem as she did? Why or why not?

_____

_____

_____

_____

THE DEVELOPING CHILD: Student Workbook

Prenatal Development

Study Guide

Directions. As you read the chapter, answer the following questions. Later, you can use this guide to study the information in the chapter.

Section 5-1: The Developing Baby

1. Define prenatal development. _____

_____

2. Define the following terms.

A. Ovum _____

_____

B. Uterus _____

_____

C. Sperm _____

_____

D. Conception _____

_____

E. Zygote _____

_____

3. Complete the following chart.

Stage	Time Span	Development That Occurs
Zygote		
Embryo		
Fetus		

(Continued on next page)

Prenatal Development   **Chapter 5 continued**

4. Explain what the placenta, amniotic fluid, and umbilical cord are and what functions they perform.

   A. Placenta _____

   _____

   _____

   B. Amniotic fluid _____

   _____

   _____

   C. Umbilical cord _____

   _____

   _____

5. What is "quickening," and when does it begin? _____

_____

_____

6. What is "lightening" and when does it begin? _____

_____

_____

Section 5-2: A Closer Look at Conception

7. What is heredity? Name three characteristics that can be hereditary. _____

_____

_____

_____

_____

8. Explain the relationship between chromosomes and genes. _____

_____

_____

_____

_____

(Continued on next page)

THE DEVELOPING CHILD: **Student Workbook**

9. Explain the difference between dominant and recessive genes. _____

_____

_____

_____

10. What determines the sex of a baby? _____

_____

_____

11. Explain how each of the following occurs:

A. Identical twins: _____

_____

_____

B. Fraternal twins: _____

_____

_____

12. Define infertility and list two causes. _____

_____

_____

13. Complete the following chart about options for infertility.

Options	Description
Adoption	
	Sperm is injected into a woman.
	An egg from the woman is removed and fertilized with sperm from the man. The resulting zygote is placed in the woman's uterus.
Ovum transfer	
Surrogate mother	

(Continued on next page)

Prenatal Development   *Chapter 5 continued*

Section 5-3: Problems in Prenatal Development

14. Explain the difference between a miscarriage and a stillbirth. _____

_____

_____

15. What is a birth defect? What proportion of children born in the United States have a birth defect?

_____

_____

_____

_____

16. Give an example of each cause of a birth defect.

    A. Environmental: _____

_____

    B. Hereditary: _____

_____

    C. Errors in chromosomes: _____

_____

17. What does a genetic counselor do? _____

_____

_____

18. Complete the following chart about prenatal tests.

Prenatal Test	Description	Risk
	Sound waves are used to make a video image of the fetus.	
Amniocentesis		
Chorionic villi sampling		

(Continued on next page)

                     THE DEVELOPING CHILD: **Student Workbook**   **45**

Section 5-4: Avoiding Dangers to the Baby

19. Differentiate between fetal alcohol syndrome and fetal alcohol effects. _____

_____

_____

20. Complete the following table with information from the chapter.

Environmental Hazard	Effect or Possible Effect	Prevention
Alcohol		Avoid alcohol during pregnancy.
Nicotine		Avoid nicotine during pregnancy.
Illegal Drugs		Avoid illegal drugs during pregnancy.
HIV	AIDS and early death	

The Developing Baby

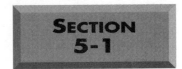

Stages of Prenatal Development

Directions. Use the timeline on the next page to fill in the events listed below. First, write the correct month in which each development takes place in the space following the description of the development. (*Events are not in the correct sequence.*) Then complete the timeline on the next page by writing the letter of the event and drawing a line from the letter to cross the timeline at the correct spot. To the *left* of the line, write in those events that happen to the developing baby. To the *right*, write in those that happen to the mother.

Developing Baby

A. Rapid weight gain continues. _____

B. Internal organs begin to form. _____

C. Fetus is about 3 inches long. _____

D. All organs are present but immature. _____

E. Breathing movements begin. _____

F. Fetus acquires antibodies from mother. _____

G. Bones begin to form. _____

Mother

H. Breasts begin to swell. _____

I. Lightening felt. _____

J. Strong fetal movements. _____

K. Appetite increases. _____

L. Missed menstrual period. _____

M. Possible backache, shortness of breath, fatigue. _____

N. Uterus is about the size of an orange. _____

(Continued on next page)

Development and Pregnancy Timeline

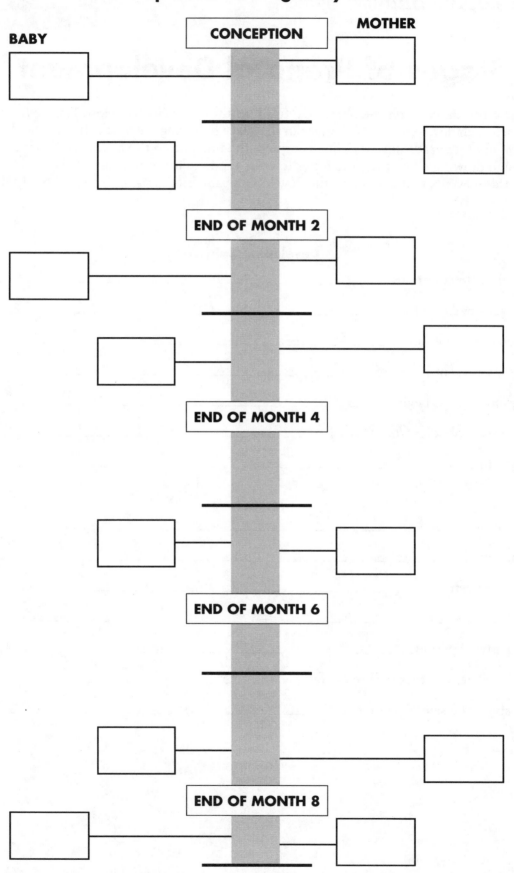

A Closer Look at Conception

Heredity in the Works

Directions. Determine the chances of passing on a genetic trait in the following situations and then complete the statements that follow.

1. The wife is blue-eyed and carries two genes for blue eyes. The husband is brown-eyed and carries one gene for brown eyes and one gene for blue eyes. Complete the grid to determine the chances that any child they have will be born with blue or with brown eyes.

		Wife	
		b	**b**
Husband	**B**		
	b		

In this diagram, the letter **B** indicates the gene for brown eyes, which is dominant. The letter **b** indicates a gene for blue eyes, which is recessive.

A. There is a _____ in four chance that any child will have brown eyes and carry genes for both brown and blue eyes.

B. There is a _____ in four chance that any child will have blue eyes and carry genes for blue eyes only.

2. The wife and husband both carry a gene for sickle-cell anemia, a disease caused by having two recessive genes. They do not have the disease but may pass it on to their children. Complete the grid to determine the chances that any child will be born with the disease.

		Wife	
		r	**n**
Husband	**r**		
	n		

In this diagram, the letter **r** indicates a gene that carries the recessive trait for sickle-cell anemia. The letter **n** indicates a normal gene—one that does not carry the sickle-cell trait.

A. There is a _____ in four chance that any child will have sickle-cell anemia and carry two genes for it.

B. There is a _____ in four chance that any child will carry a gene for sickle-cell anemia but not have the disease.

C. There is a _____ in four chance that any child will not have sickle-cell anemia or carry a gene for it.

Problems in Prenatal Development

Understanding Birth Defects

Directions. Match the description in the left-hand column to the birth defect listed in the right-hand column. Write the letter of the correct answer in the blank to the left of each description.

Description

_____ 1. An extra chromosome 21 usually causes mental retardation and abnormal physical characteristics.

_____ 2. Gap in mouth; causes problems with eating, speech, and can be corrected with surgery.

_____ 3. Affects the body's ability to process and use fat; usually causes death by age four.

_____ 4. Weakness and shrinking of the muscles; problems can be lessened with physical therapy.

_____ 5. Affects respiratory and digestive systems; treated with special diets and lung exercises.

_____ 6. Malformed red blood cells interfere with supply of oxygen; can cause tiredness and pain.

_____ 7. Body is unable to process a certain protein; can lead to mental retardation.

_____ 8. Motor system disorder caused by brain damage around the time of birth.

_____ 9. Incompletely formed spinal cord; causes partial paralysis.

Birth Defect
A. Cerebral palsy
B. Cystic fibrosis
C. Down syndrome
D. Cleft lip or palate
E. Muscular dystrophy
F. PKU
G. Sickle-cell anemia
H. Spina bifida
I. Tay-Sachs disease

Avoiding Dangers to the Baby

SECTION
5-4

Help This Unborn Child

Directions. How an expectant mother takes care of herself greatly affects prenatal development. Read each situation below. Then in the lines following, explain which of the mother's health habits may be hazardous to the unborn baby and why.

1. Dyanne is excited about the birth of her first child. However, some of the changes coming up will be hard to get used to. For example, she plans to quit smoking soon after the baby is born since she thinks it might be harmful to the child. In the meantime, Dyanne and her husband Jake look upon the pregnancy as their last chance for a long time to see their friends. Each weekend they throw a party for their friends and serve beer, which Dyanne enjoys.

_____

_____

_____

_____

_____

_____

_____

2. Earlier this week, Sandra woke up with a terrible cold. She is preparing for maternity leave and doesn't want to miss any work. She decided to take more vitamin C to help her fight the cold. She also found some nose drops in the medicine cabinet and used those to try to break up the congestion in her nasal passages. Because her body ached from the cold, she took some aspirin.

_____

_____

_____

_____

_____

_____

_____

(Continued on next page)

3. Elaine's second child is due in five months, and she is busy getting ready for the new arrival. Since she sometimes feels tired, she drinks coffee to stay awake. Each afternoon, when her first child finally settles down to a nap, she treats herself to a few brownies. Although she eats sweets, she's careful about her teeth. Just last week, she had a dental exam. The x-rays showed she had no cavities.

_____

_____

_____

_____

_____

_____

4. Marti has always had to work hard to control her weight, and she fears gaining too much weight during her pregnancy. A few years ago, a doctor had given her a prescription for amphetamines to help control her weight. She still had some pills left, so she's taking them so she won't feel so hungry. In addition, she's skipping breakfast and just having a glass of milk for lunch. Then she has a light dinner.

_____

_____

_____

_____

_____

_____

Preparing for Birth

Study Guide

Directions. As you read the chapter, answer the following questions. Later, you can use this guide to study the information in the chapter.

Section 6-1: A Healthy Pregnancy

1. List some early signs of pregnancy. Which is usually the first? _____

_____

_____

_____

_____

2. How is a pregnancy confirmed? _____

_____

3. What type of doctor specializes in care of pregnant women? How do these doctors charge for care during pregnancy and what does the fee cover?

_____

_____

_____

4. How is the due date determined? _____

_____

_____

5. List four symptoms or complications that normally occur during pregnancy. _____

_____

_____

_____

6. Natalie, who is pregnant, feels thirsty all the time. What should she do? Why? _____

_____

_____

(Continued on next page)

7. Name the basic food groups in the Food Guide Pyramid, and tell how many servings of each a pregnant woman should have every day.

_____

_____

_____

_____

_____

8. What is the recommended weight gain during pregnancy? Why is adequate weight gain important?

_____

_____

_____

_____

9. Why do you think walking, swimming, and biking are good exercises for a pregnant woman?

_____

_____

_____

_____

Section 6-2: Getting Ready for a Baby

10. What is maternity leave? How does federal law affect a woman who has a baby? _____

_____

_____

_____

_____

_____

11. Assume you are pregnant with your second child. Describe how you would tell your first child, who is three years old.

_____

_____

_____

(Continued on next page)

2. What questions should parents ask when choosing a pediatrician? _____

_____

_____

_____

_____

3. What is formula? _____

_____

_____

_____

_____

4. For each statement in the left column, identify whether breast milk or formula is more advantageous.

Advantage	Breast Milk or Formula
Babies need feeding less often.	_____
Reduces baby's risk of allergies.	_____
Reduces mother's risk of depression.	_____
Mother can take medications without worry.	_____
Best source of nutrition for baby.	_____
Allows mother a more flexible schedule.	_____
Gives baby immunity from some infections.	_____
Is free.	_____
Reduces the mother's risk of breast cancer.	_____

5. How can making a budget help expectant parents? _____

_____

_____

_____

_____

(Continued on next page)

THE DEVELOPING CHILD: Student Workbook

16. Explain the difference between fixed and flexible expenses. Give examples of each.

_____

_____

_____

_____

_____

17. Give three examples of how parents can reduce the costs of having a baby. _____

_____

_____

_____

_____

Section 6-3: Childbirth Choices

18. What is prepared childbirth? How does it benefit a pregnant woman? _____

_____

_____

_____

_____

_____

19. Differentiate between labor and delivery. _____

_____

_____

20. Describe each of the following health practitioners.

A. Obstetrician _____

_____

B. Family doctor _____

_____

_____

_____

(Continued on next page)

    C. Nurse-midwife: _____

_____

    D. Lay midwife: _____

_____

21. List three services that may be offered at a hospital with family-centered maternity care.

_____

_____

_____

_____

22. What do the initials LDRP stand for, and what does LDRP service mean? _____

_____

_____

_____

23. What is an alternative birth center? _____

_____

_____

24. List two advantages of family-centered maternity care over traditional maternity care.

_____

_____

A Healthy Pregnancy

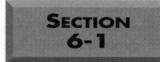

Nutrition During Pregnancy

Directions. Complete the chart below with missing information from the text. Then answer the questions that follow.

Nutrient	Functions	Source
Protein		Meat, fish, poultry, eggs, milk, cheese, beans
	Promote good health, protect against infection and disease, regulate body processes	
Minerals		
		Vegetable oils
	Provide heat and energy.	

List the four vitamins discussed in the text and give a special function for each.

_____

_____

_____

_____

Getting Ready for a Baby

Budgeting for Baby

Directions. Budgeting for a new baby requires careful planning. Read the following description of a couple preparing for their first child. Then answer the questions that follow.

Jamal and Denise are expecting their first baby. Jamal is a branch manager at a local bank and earns $2,300 per month. Denise wants to stay home and care for the baby after the birth.

The couple rents a two-bedroom apartment for $650 per month. In addition, they pay an average of $60 per month for phone expenses and $125 a month for other utilities. They've figured out they also spend $60 per month on repairs and maintenance.

Denise and Jamal have some other significant expenses. They pay $200 every month on their car loan and have 22 months yet to pay. Gas and car maintenance average another $100 a month. Car and renters' insurance cost $1200 per year. Medical insurance comes with Jamal's job, but they spend about $50 more per month on health care. While they've stopped using credit cards, they are paying off their balance with $80 each month. They put $100 in a savings account monthly.

Denise takes an exercise class that costs $10 each week. Jamal golfs, which costs the same. They also spend about $20 per week on other entertainment, such as movies, renting videos, or bowling. They spend about $50 a month on clothes and $15 a month for cleaning the clothes. Groceries run about $125 a week. Miscellaneous expenses are about $50 a month.

---

1. Use the information described above to complete the missing items in the following list. Assume that four weeks is a month.

Budget Category	Amount per Month	Budget Category	Amount per Month
Food	_____	Utilities (average)	_____
Insurance	_____	Telephone	_____
Medical care	_____	Auto loan payment	_____
Clothing and laundry	_____	Car expenses	_____
Credit card payments	_____	Home maintenance	_____
Recreation	_____	Miscellaneous	_____
Housing	_____	Savings	_____
		Total Monthly Expenses	_____

(Continued on next page)

2. Which of the categories listed above are fixed expenses? _____

_____

_____

3. Which of the categories listed above are flexible expenses? _____

_____

_____

4. Which categories are likely to see higher expenses after the baby is born? List each category and explain why you think its cost will increase.

_____

_____

_____

_____

_____

_____

5. What categories could they cut expenses to make room for these added costs? _____

_____

_____

_____

_____

_____

_____

_____

Childbirth Choices

It's Up to You

Directions. Imagine that you are twenty-five years old and married. You and your spouse are pregnant with your first child. Answer the following questions about the decisions that you would make.

1. Would you prefer to use an obstetrician, a family doctor, or a licensed midwife to deliver your baby? Why?

_____

_____

_____

2. Do you think the expectant mother should take childbirth preparation classes? Should the husband attend also? Explain your answers.

_____

_____

_____

3. Where would you choose to have the birth—a hospital with traditional maternity care, a hospital with family-centered maternity care, an alternative birth center, or at home? Why?

_____

_____

_____

4. Should the husband be in the labor and delivery room? Why or why not? _____

_____

_____

5. What would you do if your mother wanted to be in the labor and delivery room? Why?

_____

_____

(Continued on next page)

6. What arrangements would you make when the baby first came home? Would you and your spouse care for the baby alone? Would you ask for help from others in the family? Would you be willing to spend some time at another family member's home? Explain the choice you prefer.

_____

_____

_____

7. Assume that the mother had a job. Do you think she would take time off work? What about the father? Why would you make these choices?

_____

_____

_____

8. What child care arrangements would you prefer? Why? _____

_____

_____

_____

NAME _____ DATE _____ CLASS PERIOD _____

The Baby's Arrival

Study Guide

Directions. As you read the chapter, answer the following questions. Later, you can use this guide to study the information in the chapter.

Section 7-1: Labor and Birth

1. Describe two early signs of labor. _____

_____

_____

_____

2. What are contractions? How do they feel? _____

_____

_____

_____

3. How can you distinguish false labor from real contractions? _____

_____

_____

_____

_____

4. Describe the three stages of labor—what happens and how long do they last?

Stage of Labor	What Takes Place	Duration
First		
Second		
Third		

(Continued on next page)

5. What is a "breech presentation"? Why is it a complication? _____

_____

_____

_____

6. How do changes in both the mother and the baby make birth easier? _____

_____

_____

_____

_____

7. What might happen if the placenta is not delivered? _____

_____

_____

_____

8. What is a cesarean birth? _____

_____

_____

_____

9. What happens to the baby's lungs and heart after birth? _____

_____

_____

_____

10. Describe a newborn's appearance. _____

_____

_____

_____

_____

_____

(Continued on next page)

The Baby's Arrival   *Chapter 7 continued*

Section 7-2: The Postnatal Period

11. What areas are tested on the Apgar scale? _____

_____

_____

_____

12. What other tests or medical procedures are performed soon after birth? _____

_____

_____

_____

_____

13. What steps are taken to identify the baby shortly after birth? _____

_____

_____

_____

_____

14. About how long do mothers and newborns stay in the hospital? _____

_____

_____

_____

15. What do policies about bonding and rooming-in try to achieve? _____

_____

_____

_____

_____

16. What needs does a mother have after giving birth? _____

_____

_____

_____

(Continued on next page)

Section 7-3: A New Family Member

17. Describe the reflexes a baby is born with. _____

_____

_____

_____

_____

_____

_____

18. What are babies needs? _____

_____

_____

_____

_____

_____

19. How long does it take a newborn to settle into a routine? _____

_____

_____

20. How do babies communicate their needs? _____

_____

_____

Labor and Birth

Events of Labor and Birth

Directions. A normal birth progresses through three stages. Write the letter of the correct stage in the blank to the left of each description of an event.

> **STAGES OF LABOR**
>
> **A.** First stage   **B.** Second stage   **C.** Third stage

_____ **1.** Involves little or no discomfort.

_____ **2.** Episiotomy may be performed.

_____ **3.** At the beginning of this stage, contractions are about two to four minutes apart.

_____ **4.** Relaxation is important to prevent muscles from tightening.

_____ **5.** Mother may be asked to bear down to help the baby along.

_____ **6.** Shortest stage.

_____ **7.** Baby moves down into the lower pelvis and into position for birth.

_____ **8.** Near the end of this stage, contractions are strong and frequent.

_____ **9.** Longest stage.

_____ **10.** Mother may be moved from labor room to separate delivery room.

_____ **11.** Baby is born.

_____ **12.** Uterus contracts to expel placenta.

_____ **13.** Cervix dilates and becomes thinner.

_____ **14.** Forceps may be used if necessary.

The Postnatal Period

What You Need to Know About Neonatal Care

Directions. Following are the notes of a pediatrician who was scheduled to speak to a class of students about what is done in the hospital after a baby is born. The doctor was called away to another project, though, and couldn't finish his talk. Your job is to take his place, assembling his notes into an organized sequence. Some of the topics the doctor mentioned are not relevant to the subject. Cross those out before organizing your talk. Then, using the notes and the textbook, write out what you would say.

- Government funding for research on "preemies" (premature babies)
- First hour after delivery
- Apgar test and what it means
- Other tests
- Cesareans and when they're called for

- Letting mother and baby go home
- Bonding
- Stages of labor
- Identifying baby
- Helping mother start breast-feeding

_____

_____

_____

_____

_____

_____

_____

_____

_____

_____

_____

_____

_____

_____

_____

A New Family Member

Are Baby's Needs Being Met?

Directions. New parents often feel awkward caring for their new baby. Preparing for parenthood is important so that parents can recognize and meet the baby's needs. Read the example below and then answer
the questions that follow.

> Jan and Ray Strickland are parents of a boy named Reggie. The Stricklands had no special
> preparation for parenting and feel very unsure of themselves as parents.
> Reggie seems to cry constantly. Jan responds to his cries, but when he doesn't settle
> down, she gets frustrated and puts him in his crib. She loves holding Reggie when he's quiet
> and sometimes cuddles him as he falls asleep. Ray wants to do as much as possible with
> the baby, so he bathes Reggie. Since he works two jobs, though, Ray only bathes Reggie
> twice a week.
> Jan enjoys watching several daytime shows. When they're on, she doesn't talk to Reggie.
> The family is short on money, so they haven't been able to take him to the doctor, but they
> aren't worried because he's been healthy so far. They were given a mobile for Reggie's crib
> but can't afford to buy him any other toys.
> Jan and Ray are feeding the baby formula. Both parents had a weight problem during
> childhood. When Reggie started gaining weight, they decided to cut back on how much he
> was fed. They don't want their baby to have fat cheeks!

1. What basic needs of Reggie aren't being met? _____

_____

_____

2. Would parenting classes have helped the Stricklands prepare for their first child? How?

_____

_____

3. What might result from cutting back on Reggie's feeding? _____

_____

_____

_____

4. How could the Stricklands meet Reggie's need for exercise? _____

_____

_____

(Continued on next page)

THE DEVELOPING CHILD: Student Workbook   **69**

5. Why should the Stricklands try to find money to take Reggie to the doctor? _____

_____

_____

_____

6. How can Reggie's parents help his intellectual development even if they can't afford many toys?

_____

_____

_____

7. How can Reggie's parents show him that they love him? _____

_____

_____

8. How should Jan respond to Reggie's cries? _____

_____

_____

9. In light of this story, respond to the following statement: "You can't spoil newborns by giving them what they need when they need it."

_____

_____

_____

Physical Development During the First Year

Study Guide

Directions. As you read the chapter, answer the following questions. Later, you can use this guide to study the information in the chapter.

Section 8-1: Growth and Development of Infants

1. Give an example of each of the following patterns of development.

A. Head to toe: _____

_____

_____

B. Near to far: _____

_____

_____

C. Simple to complex: _____

_____

_____

2. Indicate whether the one-year-olds with the following heights and weights are average, above average, or below average.

A. 20 pounds, 4 ounces. (9.2 kg)   _____

B. 32 inches (81.3 cm)   _____

C. 18 pounds, 8 ounces (8.4 kg)   _____

D. 23 pounds (10.4 kg)   _____

E. 27 inches (68.6 cm)   _____

3. Distinguish between growth and development. _____

_____

_____

_____

(Continued on next page)

4. Explain each of the following changes in a baby's sight that takes place in the first year.

   A. Focus: _____

   _____

   _____

   _____

   B. Depth perception: _____

   _____

   _____

   C. Hand-eye coordination: _____

   _____

   _____

5. Why is babies' focus on their mouths potentially dangerous? _____

   _____

   _____

6. What symptoms may indicate that a baby is cutting teeth? _____

   _____

   _____

7. Define motor skills and give two examples. _____

   _____

   _____

8. If a child can't walk by the first birthday, does this indicate a problem? Why or why not?

   _____

   _____

Section 8-2: The Developing Brain

9. What functions of the body do the following areas of the brain control?

   A. Cortex: _____

   _____

(Continued on next page)

Physical Development During the First Year　　　　　　*Chapter 8 continued*

B. Cerebellum: _____

_____

C. Pituitary gland: _____

_____

10. Explain the role of neurotransmitters in communicating between neurons. _____

_____

_____

_____

11. Much learning comes from repetition. How does the development of connections in the brain explain why?

_____

_____

_____

12. What role does myelin play in the timing of children's learning? _____

_____

_____

_____

13. Choose one of the "rules to build a brain by." Explain what it means and give an example of how a caregiver can help a child by putting this rule in practice.

_____

_____

Section 8-3: Handling and Feeding Infants

14. What is shaken baby syndrome? What causes it? _____

_____

_____

_____

_____

(Continued on next page)

15. How often do newborns eat? Which babies tend to feed more often—those who are breastfed or those fed by bottle?

_____

_____

16. Where can a mother who breastfeeds go for advice? _____

_____

17. Explain the guidelines for bottle-feeding for each of the following areas.

A. Holding the baby: _____

_____

B. Warming the bottle: _____

_____

_____

C. Cleaning bottles and nipples: _____

_____

18. Why is it necessary to burp the baby when it is feeding? _____

_____

_____

19. About when do babies begin to eat solid food? About when are they ready for weaning?

_____

_____

20. About when are babies ready to start feeding themselves? What is the experience like?

_____

_____

_____

21. What four nutritional needs do infants have? _____

_____

_____

(Continued on next page)

Physical Development During the First Year   **Chapter 8 continued**

Section 8-4: Other Infant Care Skills

22. What must occur before a baby can have a tub bath? About when does that occur?

_____

_____

23. What part of the body should the caregiver use to test the temperature of bath water? Why? How should the water feel?

_____

_____

24. How warmly do babies need to dress? _____

_____

25. What guidelines about size should parents follow in buying clothes for babies? Why?

_____

_____

_____

_____

26. Briefly describe how to change a diaper. _____

_____

_____

27. Why should cloth diapers be laundered in hot water? _____

_____

28. How can you treat diaper rash? _____

_____

_____

29. How do a baby's sleep patterns change in a year? _____

_____

_____

30. Why is it helpful to follow the same sleep routine every night? _____

_____

_____

Growth and Development of Infants

Motor Match-Ups

Directions. In the blank to the left of each motor skill, write the letter of the *average age* at which the skill is first developed.

Motor Skills

_____ **1.** Eats with fingers.

_____ **2.** Holds head up steadily.

_____ **3.** Unsteadily reaches for objects.

_____ **4.** Lifts chin when placed on stomach.

_____ **5.** May walk alone.

_____ **6.** Rolls from side to back or back to side.

_____ **7.** Reaches for and manipulates objects with good control.

_____ **8.** Sits alone briefly.

_____ **9.** Lifts chest well above surface when placed on stomach.

_____ **10.** Picks up small objects using thumb and forefinger.

_____ **11.** Picks up large objects.

_____ **12.** Fits blocks, boxes, or nesting toys inside one another.

_____ **13.** Crawls on hands and knees.

_____ **14.** Turns completely over when laid on back or stomach.

_____ **15.** Pulls self up while holding on to furniture.

Ages
A. 1 month
B. 2 months
C. 3–4 months
D. 5–6 months
E. 7–8 months
F. 9–10 months
G. 11–12 months

The Developing Brain

Helping the Brain Develop

Directions. The environment that parents provide for their children greatly affects how the children's brain develops. Read each situation below. Then in the lines following, say whether the parents' actions were wise or not and explain why.

1. Renee wants her seven-year-old daughter Traci to have all the advantages that she didn't have in her own childhood. She has Traci taking dance lessons, learning how to program the computer, playing on the local soccer team, and singing in the choir.

_____

_____

_____

_____

2. "I don't know what to do," Alan said to his father. Alan was the father of a two-year-old, and he often spoke to his father looking for advice about raising his child. "We've been hoping that we could teach Sean to read early so he would have a head start when he's ready for school. We've tried to teach him the letters of the alphabet using blocks, but he only throws the blocks around or stacks them into towers."

_____

_____

_____

3. Audra patiently picked the ball up and brought it back to little Emily, even though she had done it many times before. Sure enough, as soon as Emily had the ball, she threw it again. Audra retrieved it one more time and handed it over. The game continued for another ten minutes until Emily finally tired of it. Audra sat down with a sigh.

_____

_____

_____

(Continued on next page)

4. Six-year-old Teddy was in tears. "I hate it. I hate playing soccer. I never liked it. I never will like it." He stomped his feet. "But you always seemed happy when we went to games," his mother said. "I wasn't happy. But you wanted me to play. So I did. Please don't make me play again this year." "OK," his mother said. "It's for you to choose. If you don't want to play, you don't have to."

_____

_____

5. Four-year-old Tara was sitting on the floor trying to work out a jigsaw puzzle. Her father was watching. She seemed to be stumped. After several moments, her father reached over and put a piece in, saying "See, honey, it goes here with the others like it." Then he finished up the puzzle and said "Here's what it looks like when it's finished."

_____

_____

_____

_____

6. As Consuelo did her shopping, she kept up a running commentary. One-year-old Pepe, sitting in the shopping cart, heard everything his mother said. When she told him to feel how round the oranges were, he reached out. When she said that the milk container was cold, he touched that too.

_____

_____

_____

_____

Handling and Feeding Infants

Healthy Care for Babies

Directions. Read the following statements about handling babies. If the action described is healthy, write an **H** in the space to the left of the description. If it is unhealthy, write a **U** in that space. In the lines below the statement, explain why.

_____ **1.** Kevin's father likes to rock the baby every night before bed.

_____

_____

_____ **2.** Karen is tired of breast-feeding. She has started her two-month-old eating solid food, hoping that he'll not nurse as much.

_____

_____

_____ **3.** Martina put Stevie into his crib at bedtime. "Here's your bottle, sweetie. If you get hungry, you can have something." Then she put the nipple of the bottle into Stevie's mouth.

_____

_____

_____ **4.** Jason was in a hurry to feed the baby so he put the bottle in the microwave. "I know this isn't great," he said to himself. "But I'll just set it for 30 seconds so he won't get hurt."

_____

_____

_____ **5.** Tori was excited. Her daughter was finally going to start eating fruit! She opened the jar and carefully spooned a bit of the applesauce into a small bowl. Putting a little bit on a spoon, she smiled and said, "Here we go, kiddo. Down the hatch!"

_____

_____

_____

(Continued on next page)

_____   **6.** Brooke laughed at what her friend had said. "No, I don't find breast-feeding to be embarrassing or difficult. It's easier than fiddling with all the bottles and stuff. We're doing fine."

_____

_____

_____   **7.** Marvin was so frustrated. His daughter wouldn't stop crying. Night after night, she cried. The more he tried to calm her, the more tense her body felt in his arms. Shaking her, he shouted "You've got to stop!"

_____

_____

_____   **8.** Todd had his lips closed tightly as though he didn't want to eat. His father brought another spoonful of cereal to his son's mouth. "Come on, little one. You're looking awful scrawny. You need to put some meat on your bones. Eat up!"

_____

_____

_____   **9.** After his little baby had fed for a while, Sterling took the bottle away and put it on the table. "You can have some more in a minute, baby," he said. "First, though, Daddy needs to burp you."

_____

_____

_____   **10.** Rose put the empty baby's bottle in the sink with the other dishes. "I'll wash it later," she thought.

_____

_____

Other Infant Care Skills

Smart Shopping for Baby

Directions. Read each of the product labels below. Then, in the spaces provided, tell (A) whether the item is useful in infant care; (B) if not, why not; and (C) if so, what function it serves.

1.

BACTISPORICIN OINTMENT
Now improved.
Contains zinc oxide for cooling relief.
Use as directed. Net wt. 1 oz. {28.4g}

2.

R-Tip Swabs
New special design makes these just right for "little" places, such as baby's ears and nose.
375 Safety Swabs

3.

WeeChums brand overalls. Made for the active lifestyle of your toddler. Improved E-Z open snaps, reinforced knee.

4.

Cap-Away
The lotion made specially for cradle cap. Contains secret ingredients found in no other product. Your baby will love it—and so will you!
6 fl. oz.

1. A. _____

   B. _____

   C. _____

2. A. _____

   B. _____

   C. _____

3. A. _____

   B. _____

   C. _____

4. A. _____

   B. _____

   C. _____

Emotional and Social Development During the First Year

Study Guide

Directions. As you read the chapter, answer the following questions. Later, you can use this guide to study the information in the chapter.

Section 9-1: Understanding Emotional and Social Development

1. Distinguish between emotional and social development. _____

_____

_____

_____

_____

2. How are emotional and social development related? _____

_____

_____

3. What have studies shown about the importance of personal care and touching to babies? Give specific examples.

_____

_____

_____

_____

_____

4. What is failure to thrive? How can the effects be reversed? _____

_____

_____

_____

_____

(Continued on next page)

Emotional and Social Development During the First Year   *Chapter 9 continued*

5. How does responding to a baby's needs build trust? _____

_____

_____

6. Explain the importance of emotional climate to a baby's development. _____

_____

_____

_____

7. What is temperament? _____

_____

_____

8. Match the description with the way of looking at temperament by writing the appropriate letter from the box below in the space before the description.

WAYS OF LOOKING AT TEMPERAMENT

A. Perceptiveness	**D.** Adaptability	**G.** Sensitivity
B. Mood	**E.** Energy	**H.** First reaction
C. Intensity	**F.** Persistence	**I.** Regularity

Descriptions

_____ Strength or weakness of a child's emotional responses to events and to other people.

_____ Child's determination to complete an action.

_____ Child with strong reactions to his or her own feelings.

_____ Child who is very aware of the world and can become easily distracted by new things.

_____ Child who easily adjusts to changes.

_____ Child who follows set patterns day in and day out.

_____ Child who is physically very active.

_____ Based on how children respond when faced with a new situation.

_____ How positive or negative a child generally is.

(Continued on next page)

Section 9-2: Emotional and Social Development of Infants

9. Baby Andre had grabbed the family cat by the tail and was pulling on it. "No, Andre, that's not how we treat the cat," his mother said sharply. While she did, Andre's father said, "Look at the funny expression on the cat's face" and laughed. How might Andre respond to these messages?

_____

_____

_____

_____

10. About when do the following emotions appear?

Emotion	When It Appears
Distress	
Anger	
Affection	
Fear of strangers	
Delight	
Disgust	

11. What is the first thing to do when responding to a crying baby? _____

_____

_____

_____

12. How can you comfort a crying baby who needs emotional support? _____

_____

_____

_____

13. How can babies comfort themselves? _____

_____

_____

_____

(Continued on next page)

Emotional and Social Development During the First Year   *Chapter 9 continued*

14. What is colic? What can parents do about it? _____

_____

_____

_____

15. Identify at what age each of the following milestones of social development typically takes place.

A. Babies smile and watch people move about: _____

B. Babies prefer parents over others: _____

C. Babies like to be the center of attention: _____

D. Babies prefer to be with other people: _____

E. Babies want companionship as well as physical care: _____

F. Babies first respond to voices: _____

16. How is stranger anxiety linked to intellectual development? _____

_____

_____

_____

_____

Understanding Emotional and Social Development

Testing Temperament

Directions. Read the following components of temperament. Then use the scale on the next page to rate yourself in each area by putting a checkmark (✔) in the space that seems to match you. When you're done, answer the question that follows.

COMPONENTS OF TEMPERAMENT

Intensity: How intensely do you react? If you laugh softly, you are less intense. If you laugh loudly, you are more intense. Do you respond to frustration mildly or with great force?

Persistence: How do you respond when asked to stop doing something? If you insist on finishing, you are high in persistence. If you easily set it aside, you are low in persistence.

Sensitivity: People who are easily bothered by noises, temperature, the taste of food, or the tags on clothing are high in sensitivity. Those who aren't affected are low in sensitivity.

Perceptiveness: If you notice what people wear or where objects are, you are high in perceptiveness. If you are not attuned to your surroundings, you are low in this trait.

Adaptability: If you're annoyed when plans change or if you find it difficult to get started on a new project, you're low in adaptability. If you can move smoothly from one task to another, you are highly adaptable.

Regularity: If you like things the same way all the time, you are highly regular. If you prefer change and new experiences, you are low in regularity.

Energy: How quiet or active are you? A highly energetic person is always on the move and expresses feelings in physical ways. A low-energy person is generally quiet and not very physical.

First Reaction: How do you respond to new situations and activities? You might feel very uncomfortable or hold back, preferring to watch others before you join in. You might dive right in, eager to get started or to get to know new people.

Mood: What is your general outlook on life: are you generally a positive, happy person or a negative, unpleasant person?

(Continued on next page)

Understanding Emotional and Social Development   *Section 9-1 continued*

	Low Intensity		High Intensity	
Intensity	1	2	3	4	5

	Low Persistence		High Persistence	
Persistence	1	2	3	4	5

	Low Sensitivity		High Sensitivity	
Sensitivity	1	2	3	4	5

	Low Perceptiveness		High Perceptiveness	
Perceptiveness	1	2	3	4	5

	High Adaptability		Low Adaptability	
Adaptability	1	2	3	4	5

	High Regularity		Low Regularity	
Regularity	1	2	3	4	5

	Low Energy		High Energy	
Energy	1	2	3	4	5

	First Reaction: Dives in		First Reaction: Stays back	
First Reaction	1	2	3	4	5

	Mood: Positive		Mood: Negative	
Mood	1	2	3	4	5

Based on how you rated yourself, how would you describe your temperament?

_____

_____

_____

_____

Emotional and Social Development of Infants

Stages of Emotional and Social Development

Directions. Use the timeline on the next page to fill in the events listed below. First, write the correct month in which each development takes place in the space following the description of the development. (*Events are not in the correct sequence.*) Then complete the timeline on the next page by writing the letter of the event and drawing a line from the letter to cross the timeline at the correct spot. To the *left* of the line, write in signs of emotional development. To the *right* of the line, write in signs of social development.

Emotional Development

A. Babies show distress. _____

B. Babies show elation. _____

C. Babies begin to show their dislikes. _____

D. Babies smile to show delight. _____

E. Babies show affection. _____

F. Babies begin to fear strangers. _____

G. Babies show anger when they can't have their own way. _____

Social Development

H. Babies turn their heads in response to a voice. _____

I. Babies begin to tolerate strangers. _____

J. Babies enjoy games like peekaboo. _____

K. Babies stop crying when lifted or touched. _____

L. Babies cry when left alone in a room. _____

M. Babies may crawl into a room to be with others. _____

N. Babies enjoy games involving chasing. _____

(Continued on next page)

NAME _____ DATE _____ CLASS PERIOD _____

Emotional and Social Development of Infants   *Section 9-2 continued*

Emotional and Social Development Timeline

Emotional Development   **Social Development**

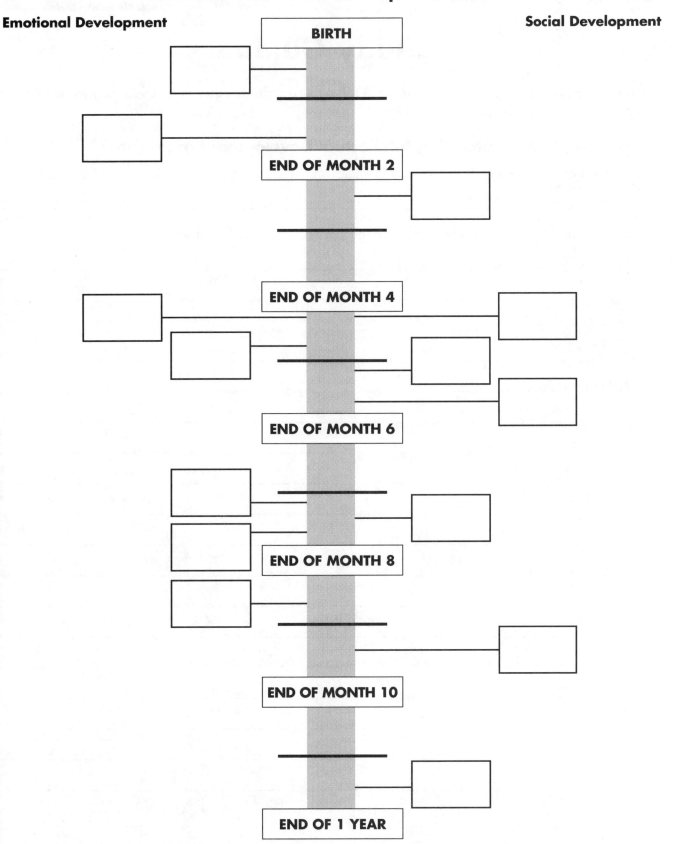

Intellectual Development
During the First Year

Study Guide

Directions. As you read the chapter, answer the following questions. Later, you can use this guide to study the information in the chapter.

Section 10-1: Understanding Intellectual Development of Infants

1. How is perception related to learning? _____

_____

2. Give examples of the four abilities that babies develop in their first year.

A. Memory: _____

_____

_____

_____

B. Associations: _____

_____

_____

C. Understanding cause and effect: _____

_____

_____

D. Attention span: _____

_____

_____

3. What two principles of intellectual development did Piaget discover? _____

_____

_____

_____

_____

(Continued on next page)

4. Fill in the following chart with information about Piaget's four periods of intellectual development.

Period	Age	Description
Sensorimotor		
	2 years to 7 years	
		Learns best through direct experience; logical thinking possible; can classify objects.
Formal operations		

5. Define object permanence. During which of Piaget's periods is this concept learned?

_____

_____

_____

6. How do children solve problems in the preoperational period? _____

_____

7. What is symbolic thinking? How does it relate to how a three-year-old learns? _____

_____

_____

_____

8. What criticisms do other experts offer of Piaget's ideas? _____

_____

_____

Section 10-2: Helping Babies Learn

9. How does caring for a child help mental abilities develop? _____

_____

_____

_____

_____

(Continued on next page)

10. What are five ways that caregivers can encourage learning? _____

_____

_____

11. Why is safety an important issue in a baby's intellectual development? _____

_____

_____

_____

12. Give an example of a toy that is good for a twelve-month-old but not for a four-month-old. Explain why it is suitable for one age but not the other.

_____

_____

_____

_____

_____

13. Why are toys important in intellectual development? _____

_____

_____

14. How do babies communicate before they can use words? _____

_____

_____

15. How does babbling help a baby learn language? _____

_____

_____

16. Describe speech milestones at each of the following ages:

   A. Birth to 6 months: _____

   B. 7 to 12 months: _____

   C. 13 to 18 months: _____

   D. 18 months to 2 years: _____

   E. 2 to 3 years: _____

Understanding Intellectual Development
of Infants

Applying Piaget's Work

Directions. The chart below shows the stages and characteristics of intellectual development that Piaget placed in the sensorimotor period—the first of the periods he identified. In the right column, write in examples of activities or objects that could be given infants at each stage in order to match its characteristics.

Piaget's Sensorimotor Period

Ages	Characteristics	Activities or Objects
Birth to one month	• Practice inborn reflexes. • Does not understand self as a separate person.	
One to four months	• Combines two or more reflexes. • Develops hand-mouth coordination.	
Four to eight months	• Acts intentionally to produce results. • Improves hand-eye coordination.	
Eight to twelve months	• Begins to solve problems. • Finds partially hidden objects. • Imitates others.	
Twelve to eighteen months	• Finds hidden objects. • Explores and experiments. • Understands that objects exist independently.	
Eighteen to twenty-four months	• Solves problems by thinking through sequences. • Can think using symbols. • Begins imaginative thinking.	

Helping Babies Learn

Toy Evaluation

Directions. Select a toy that might be appropriate for a child between seven and twelve months old. You may select one from those you see in stores, catalogs, or magazines, or one that belongs to your family or someone you know. Write the name of the toy below. Draw or paste a picture of it on another sheet of paper. Then answer the questions that follow.

Name of the toy: _____

1. What appeals to you about this toy? _____

_____

_____

2. Is it a safe toy for a baby to play with? Why or why not? _____

_____

_____

3. Would it be easy to keep clean? Explain. _____

_____

_____

4. What materials are used in making this toy? _____

_____

_____

5. Is it durable and well constructed? Explain. _____

_____

_____

6. Check the information in the textbook about appropriate toys for children these ages. Would this toy really interest a child this age, or would it appeal more to adults? Explain.

_____

_____

(Continued on next page)

Helping Babies Learn   *Section 10-2 continued*

7. Does the toy encourage problem solving? Why or why not? _____

_____

_____

8. What skills does the toy teach? _____

_____

_____

9. Would this toy stimulate a child's imagination or creativity? Why or why not? _____

_____

_____

10. Could this toy be used in cooperative play? If so, how? _____

_____

_____

11. Does the toy encourage interaction between children and adults? If so, how? _____

_____

_____

12. Can you think of any household objects that could substitute for this toy? Explain. _____

_____

_____

13. How many months do you think a child would enjoy this toy? Explain. _____

_____

_____

Physical Development from One to Three

Study Guide

Directions. As you read the chapter, answer the following questions. Later, you can use this guide to study the information in the chapter.

Section 11-1: Physical Growth and Development from One to Three

1. What is a toddler? _____

_____

_____

2. Fill in the following chart with the missing information.

	Age One	**Age Two**	**Age Three**
Average Height	29.8 inches, or 75.7 cm		
Average Weight		27.7 lbs, or 12.6 kg	
Proportion			Chest is larger than head and abdomen. Arms, legs, and trunk continue to grow rapidly.
Posture		Child stands up straighter but not completely erect.	
Number of Teeth			20
Large Motor Skills (one example)			
Small Motor Skills (one example)			

(Continued on next page)

Physical Development from One to Three   *Chapter 11 continued*

3. List two factors that control the quality of children's teeth. _____

_____

_____

4. Are tasks developmentally appropriate for all children at a certain age? Explain why or why not.

_____

_____

_____

_____

_____

Section 11-2: Caring for Children from One to Three

5. Compare the self-feeding abilities of one-, two-, and three-year-olds. _____

_____

_____

_____

_____

6. Give examples of each of the five ways to make foods interesting for children.

A. Color: _____

_____

B. Texture: _____

_____

C. Shape: _____

_____

D. Temperature: _____

_____

E. Ease of eating: _____

_____

(Continued on next page)

THE DEVELOPING CHILD: **Student Workbook**

7. Read the following three descriptions and state whether the child in each example is probably one, two, or three years old. Write the child's age in the space to the left of the description.

_____ **A.** After washing the rest of his body, Henry called his father to wash his back. He asks his father to dry his back also.

_____ **B.** Chan's mother told him it was time to take his bath. While she folded laundry in the bathroom, he washed and dried himself.

_____ **C.** Carlota rubbed the washcloth over her stomach and said proudly, "I wash me." Her mother told her she had done a good job.

8. Read the following three descriptions and state whether the child in each example is probably one, two, or three years old. Write the child's age in the space to the left of the description.

_____ **A.** Antonio's mother told him it was time to dress. He put on all his clothes, including his shoes, which had tape-and-loop fasteners.

_____ **B.** "You know what Clarysse did today?" the girl's father told her mother. "When I was dressing her, she put her arms through the sleeves. Isn't that great!"

_____ **C.** Nadia could put her pants on but had to ask her sister for help with her shirt.

9. Name and describe three important characteristics to look for in children's clothing.

_____

_____

_____

_____

_____

_____

_____

_____

10. How do nap patterns change in these years? _____

_____

_____

_____

_____

_____

(Continued on next page)

Physical Development from One to Three   *Chapter 11 continued*

11. What types of disturbances might a child experience in sleeping patterns? _____

_____

_____

_____

_____

12. What shows a child's readiness to begin toilet training? _____

_____

_____

_____

_____

13. What typically comes first, bladder or bowel control? How far apart are these two aspects of toilet training?

_____

_____

_____

_____

Physical Growth and Development from One to Three

Identifying Ages

Directions. The pictures below show children of different ages in action. For each picture, identify the child's approximate age—one, two, or three—and explain why.

1.

_____
_____
_____
_____
_____

3.

_____
_____
_____
_____
_____

2.

_____
_____
_____
_____
_____

4.

_____
_____
_____
_____
_____

Caring for Children from One to Three

Planning Meals for Children

Directions. Listed below are four menus for toddlers. Using information from Section 11-2, evaluate the meals to identify ways they could be improved. In the spaces below the menus, list at least two problems you see or suggestions you can make to improve the menus. Then complete the rest of the activity.

<table>
<tr><td>

Menu A
Fried hamburger on a bun
French fries
Fried apple pies
Milk

</td><td>

Menu B
Meat loaf
Mashed potatoes
Applesauce
Grits
Vanilla pudding
Milk

</td></tr>
<tr><td>

Menu C
Meatballs
Green beans
Brussels sprouts
Dinner rolls
Dip of lime sherbet
Milk

</td><td>

Menu D
Baked trout
Baked potato
Stuffed acorn squash
Garlic bread
Milk

</td></tr>
</table>

Evaluation

1. Menu A: _____

_____

2. Menu B: _____

_____

3. Menu C: _____

_____

4. Menu D: _____

_____

(Continued on next page)

THE DEVELOPING CHILD: Student Workbook

5. How would you change two of these menus to make them more suitable for a child one to three years old? Make your new menus by crossing out and adding to the menus on the previous page. Bear in mind that you can change the type of food, the method of cooking, or the way of serving the food. In the lines below, explain why you made the changes.

_____

_____

_____

6. In the space below, plan a dinner menu for a three-year-old. Specify serving sizes. Then evaluate the menu by circling either "Yes" or "No" to the left of the questions that follow.

Food   **Serving Sizes**

_____   _____

_____   _____

_____   _____

_____   _____

_____   _____

_____   _____

Yes   No   **A.** Are all food groups from the Food Guide Pyramid represented?

Yes   No   **B.** Are the serving sizes appropriate for a three-year-old?

Yes   No   **C.** Does the meal contain a variety of colors?

Yes   No   **D.** Are the food textures varied?

Yes   No   **E.** Are the food shapes varied?

Yes   No   **F.** Can the foods be eaten easily by a three-year-old?

Yes   No   **G.** Does the menu avoid having too many strong flavors that a child might not like?

*Emotional and Social Development
from One to Three*

Study Guide

Directions. As you read the chapter, answer the following questions. Later, you can use this guide to study the information in the chapter.

Section 12-1: Emotional Development from One to Three

1. Why are children self-centered at eighteen months? _____

_____

_____

2. Identify and describe three causes for the negativism of children around eighteen months?

_____

_____

_____

_____

_____

_____

3. Identify which ages—eighteen months, two years, two and one-half years, three years, three and one-half years—are generally calmer and which generally have more frustrations.

  A. Calmer: _____

  _____

  B. More frustrations: _____

  _____

4. How does anger in an eighteen month old differ from anger in a three year old? _____

_____

_____

_____

_____

_____

(Continued on next page)

5. Anger, fear, and jealousy can be more common in some children than others. Besides temperament, what factors might cause some children to exhibit these emotions more than others?

_____

_____

_____

_____

_____

6. What is separation anxiety and how can parents try to minimize it? _____

_____

_____

_____

_____

7. Give an example of sibling rivalry. _____

_____

_____

_____

8. Explain how a parent can help a child develop a positive self-concept. _____

_____

_____

_____

_____

Section 12-2: Social Development from One to Three

9. What is socialization? How does children's socialization change over time? _____

_____

_____

_____

_____

_____

(Continued on next page)

Emotional and Social Development from One to Three   *Chapter 12 continued*

10. Describe the two different ways in which children play with other children. At what ages do children engage in these two types of play?

_____

_____

_____

_____

_____

_____

11. Describe the behavior of children from two to three and one-half in terms of their concern with pleasing others.

A. Two: _____

_____

_____

_____

B. Two and one-half: _____

_____

_____

_____

C. Three: _____

_____

_____

_____

D. Three and one-half: _____

_____

_____

_____

(Continued on next page)

12. Why is it beneficial to a child to have companions of the same age rather than just adult companionship?

_____

_____

_____

_____

_____

_____

13. What would you say to a parent who wished to put an end to her child's playing with an imaginary friend?

_____

_____

_____

_____

14. Match the methods for dealing with inappropriate behavior with the age when the method is an appropriate strategy by writing the letter of the method in the space to the left of the age.

Age

_____ Eight to twelve months

_____ Twelve to fifteen months

_____ Fifteen to twenty-four months

_____ Two to three years

_____ Three to four years

Methods for Handling

A. Distraction, removal, and spoken restrictions
B. Distraction and physical removal
C. Distraction
D. Reasonable, loving guidance
E. Spoken commands with explanation

15. How can caregivers promote sharing among young children? _____

_____

_____

_____

_____

Emotional Development from One to Three

Solving the Puzzle of Emotional Development

Directions. Unscramble the terms in the list below and match them to the definitions. Write the correct term in the space provided.

SCRAMBLED TERMS

A. oevl   **E.** pymteah   **I.** glibisn viyrlar

B. raneg   **F.** vitsmegani   **J.** lefs-dreneect

C. oaeljuys   **G.** reetpm mtuanrt

D. tesanroipa yetanix   **H.** refa

_____ **1.** An emotion two-year-olds often express by crying and screaming.

_____ **2.** An emotion that can protect a child from dangerous situations.

_____ **3.** A release of violent anger or frustration by violent screaming, crying, or kicking.

_____ **4.** Thinking about one's own wants and needs but not those of other people.

_____ **5.** Doing the opposite of what others want, which is a normal part of the development of children from one to three.

_____ **6.** Fear of being away from parents, familiar caregivers, or the normal environment.

_____ **7.** The ability to put oneself in another's place.

_____ **8.** Competition between brothers or sisters for their parents' affection and attention.

_____ **9.** Common emotion that is evident after the first year and which may result from resenting affection between parents.

_____ **10.** An emotion first expressed toward those who satisfy a baby's physical needs.

Social Development from One to Three

Guiding a Child to Desirable Behavior

Directions. In each of the following situations, explain how the child can be guided to more desirable behavior, taking into consideration the child's age, environment, and temperament.

1. For a holiday, three-year-old Johnny and his two-year-old brother Randy both received coloring books. Randy liked the characters in his brother's coloring book and tried to take it. Johnny got mad and tried to get it back. Their parents heard the argument and came to see what was happening.

_____

_____

_____

_____

_____

2. Stacey, who is four, was playing with blocks at her child care center. Another child the same age came to the block area and began to play also. Stacey protested that the blocks were for her to play with. One of the center's staff heard them talking.

_____

_____

_____

_____

3. Megan and her neighbor Sondra are playing in the sandbox in Megan's back yard while Megan's father watches them. They are both eighteen months old. Sondra reaches for a toy that Megan wants. She pushes Sondra and grabs the toy herself. Sondra falls down into the sandbox and starts to cry.

_____

_____

_____

_____

_____

(Continued on next page)

Social Development from One to Three

4. Charlie, who is two, and Carrie, who is three, are at the pool with their mother. She is taking turns giving them rides around the pool. Carrie gets mad because she says Charlie has gotten more rides than she has.

_____

_____

_____

_____

5. Ben, who is almost two, has gotten into the emergency candle drawer where his parents keep matches. His father catches him.

_____

_____

_____

_____

_____

THE DEVELOPING CHILD: Student Workbook

Intellectual Development from One to Three

Study Guide

Directions. As you read the chapter, answer the following questions. Later, you can use this guide to study the information in the chapter.

Section 13-1: Understanding Learning and the Mind

1. Define intelligence. _____

_____

_____

_____

_____

2. What features of a child's environment can promote intelligence? _____

_____

_____

_____

3. Give examples of each of the four methods of learning.

A. Incidental learning: _____

_____

B. Trial and error: _____

_____

C. Imitation: _____

_____

D. Directed learning: _____

_____

4. How do children organize the information they receive from the outside world? _____

_____

_____

(Continued on next page)

5. Name some categories that children put concepts into. _____

_____

_____

6. Which two intellectual activities do you feel are most closely related? Explain how they are related.

_____

_____

_____

_____

7. Compare a baby's ability to concentrate to an adult's. _____

_____

_____

_____

_____

8. How can parents help improve their children's perception? _____

_____

_____

_____

9. What stages of problem solving does a child go through? _____

_____

_____

_____

_____

10. What are some products of a child's creativity? _____

_____

_____

_____

(Continued on next page)

THE DEVELOPING CHILD: Student Workbook   **111**

11. How could curiosity be mistaken for misbehavior? _____

_____

_____

Section 13-2: Encouraging Learning from One to Three

12. Name what you think are the two most important ways in which a caregiver can guide the learning of a child and explain why they are so important.

_____

_____

_____

13. What is the most important consideration when buying toys? Why? _____

_____

_____

14. Name the other considerations. _____

_____

_____

_____

15. How is children's language development influenced by how others speak to them? _____

_____

_____

16. What can a parent do if a child has trouble speaking? _____

_____

_____

_____

_____

Understanding Learning and the Mind

Planning Activities

Directions. Use the chart below to write down an activity, toy, or game that could be played with children from one to three to promote each intellectual ability listed.

Ability	Activity, Toy, or Game
Attention	
Categorizing	
Creativity	
Curiosity	
Imagination	
Memory	
Perception	
Reasoning	

THE DEVELOPING CHILD: Student Workbook

Encouraging Learning from One to Three

**SECTION
13-2**

Writing About Children

Directions. You are the editor of a magazine for parents. Your staff has given you several ideas for articles, which are listed below. Cross out any ideas that you think are poor ones and, in the spaces below, explain why. For the ideas that you think are good, write down the main points that the article should cover.

1. "Teach Your Two-Year-Old How to Read" _____

_____

_____

2. "Parents as Teachers" _____

_____

_____

_____

3. "The Year's Best Toys" _____

_____

_____

_____

4. "How to Keep the Toddlers from Interrupting" _____

_____

_____

5. "How to Talk to Your Child" _____

_____

_____

_____

Physical Development from Four to Six

Study Guide

Directions. As you read the chapter, answer the following questions. Later, you can use this guide to study the information in the chapter.

Section 14-1: Physical Growth and Development from Four to Six

1. Describe how children's average height and weight change from ages four to six. _____

_____

_____

_____

_____

2. Describe how a child's body shape changes from ages four to six. _____

_____

_____

_____

_____

3. Which permanent teeth appear first? What is their role in the arrangement of the teeth in the mouth?

_____

_____

_____

4. Paul Sanders is annoyed because his son, five years old, sucks his thumb. What advice would you give to the father?

_____

_____

_____

_____

(Continued on next page)

5. For each skill listed in the chart below, decide whether it is a small or large motor skill and identify the age—four, five, or six—when a child typically learns it.

Ability	Large or Small	Approximate Age
Writes entire words		
Skips, alternating feet		
Laces shoes		
Ties shoelaces		
Buttons, snaps, zips clothing		
Throws overhand		
Rides a bicycle		
Gallops and hops		
Dresses and undresses self		
Balances on tiptoe		
Builds block towers up to shoulder height		
Throws ball accurately		

6. Define ambidextrous. _____

_____

7. By what age is handedness apparent? What are some theories of how it develops?

_____

_____

_____

_____

Section 14-2: Providing Care for Children from Four to Six

8. Should a child four to six be given food portions as large as an adult? Who should eat more often, a child or an adult? Why?

_____

_____

_____

_____

(Continued on next page)

Physical Development from Four to Six   **Chapter 14 continued**

9. Zach is small for his age, often has a cold, and has a hard time keeping focused in school. What might be his problem?

_____

_____

10. What are the three steps parents can take to encourage their children to develop good eating habits?

_____

_____

_____

_____

11. Why might bath time be more difficult with children aged four to six? _____

_____

_____

_____

12. You're the parent of Lisa, a five-year-old who just came back from a checkup at the dentist that showed she had healthy teeth with no cavities. You're talking to your neighbor, who also has a five-year-old girl. That child just had two cavities. Your neighbor says, "I don't understand why your daughter's checkup was so much better." What would you advise your neighbor to do?

_____

_____

_____

_____

13. Vicki never fussed about her clothing, but since her sixth birthday she's refused to wear certain outfits. What might cause that?

_____

_____

_____

14. Before taking her son anywhere, Elizabeth Connolly reminds him to go to the bathroom. If they arrive at a place he's never been before, she makes sure he knows where the bathroom is before he starts any activities. What problem are these steps aimed at handling?

_____

_____

(Continued on next page)

THE DEVELOPING CHILD: **Student Workbook**

15. What steps can children take to care for their own clothing? What can parents do to make these activities easier for the child?

_____

_____

_____

_____

16. What are the sleep habits of children these ages? _____

_____

_____

_____

_____

Physical Growth and Development from Four to Six

Describing Growth and Development

Directions. Dr. Janna Pavlev, a pediatrician and author, is giving an illustrated lecture to parents about the growth and development of preschoolers. You are Dr. Pavlev's assistant. Listed below are descriptions of some of the slides that Dr. Pavlev will show during her lecture. In the lines below each description, write some notes that Dr. Pavlev can use as the basis for her talk.

1. Slide: A group of preschoolers standing together in class photo. Children are of different heights and weights.

_____

_____

_____

_____

2. Slide: Six-year-old boy standing next to two-year-old boy at backyard pool; both are in swimsuits so body shapes are evident.

_____

_____

_____

_____

3. Slide: Six-year-old girl smiling at camera missing two lower front teeth. _____

_____

_____

_____

_____

4. Slide: Children aged four to six running in park or playground. _____

_____

_____

_____

_____

THE DEVELOPING CHILD: Student Workbook **119**

Providing Care for Children from Four to Six

Reading Nutrition Labels

Direction. All commercially prepared cereals have nutrition labels on the sides or backs of the boxes. Two cereal labels are reproduced here. Read each label, and then answer the questions that follow.

Label A

1. How big is a serving?

   Cereal A _____

   Cereal B _____

2. How many servings are in a box?

   Cereal A _____   Cereal B _____

3. How many calories are in each serving, both plain and with milk?

   Cereal A plain _____   Cereal B plain _____

   Cereal A with milk _____   Cereal B with milk _____

4. What are the four main ingredients (the first four listed) in each cereal?

   Cereal A _____

   _____

   Cereal B _____

   _____

   _____

5. Would either of these cereals be a good source of vitamin C? Explain why or why not.

   Cereal A _____

   _____

   _____

   Cereal B _____

   _____

   _____

Nutrition Facts

Serving Size   3/4 Cup (31g/1.1 oz)
Servings per Container   18

Amount Per Serving	Cereal	Cereal with ½ Cup Vitamins A & D Skim Milk
Calories	120	160
Fat Calories	0	0

	% Daily Value**	
Total Fat 0g*	0%	0%
Saturated Fat 0g	0%	0%
Polyunsaturated Fat 0g		
Monounsaturated Fat 0g		
Cholesterol 0mg	0%	0%
Sodium 210mg	9%	11%
Potassium 20mg	1%	6%
Total Carbohydrate 28g	9%	11%
Dietary Fiber 0g	0%	0%
Sugars 13g		
Other Carbohydrate 15g		
Protein 1g		

Vitamin A	15%	20%
Vitamin C	25%	25%
Calcium	0%	15%
Iron	10%	10%
Vitamin D	10%	25%
Thiamin	25%	30%
Riboflavin	25%	35%
Niacin	25%	25%
Vitamin B6	25%	25%
Folate	25%	25%

*Amount in cereal. One half cup skim milk contributes an additional 40 calories, 65mg sodium, 6g total carbohydrate (6g sugars), and 4g protein.
**Percent Daily Values are based on a 2,000 calorie diet. Your daily values may be higher or lower depending on your calorie needs:

		Calories	2,000	2,500
Total Fat	Less than		65g	80g
Sat. Fat	Less than		20g	25g
Cholesterol	Less than		300mg	300mg
Sodium	Less than		2,400mg	2,400mg
Potassium			3,500mg	3,500mg
Total Carbohydrate			300mg	375g
Dietary Fiber			25g	30g

Calories per gram:
Fat 9 • Carbohydrate 4 • Protein 4

Ingredients: Corn, sugar, salt, malt flavoring, corn syrup.
Vitamins and Iron: ascorbic acid, (vitamin C), niacinamide, iron, pyridoxine hydrochloride (vitamin B6) riboflavin (vitamin B2), vitamin A palmitate (protected with BHT), thiamin hydrochloride (vitamin B1), folic acid, and vitamin D.

(Continued on next page)

Label B

6. Would either of these cereals be a good choice for a low-sugar diet? Explain why or why not.

Cereal A _____

_____

_____

Cereal B _____

_____

_____

7. Why should children be encouraged to eat these cereals with milk?

_____

_____

_____

8. Which cereal has more fat? _____

_____

_____

_____

9. Which cereal is a better source of iron? _____

_____

_____

_____

_____

10. Would you serve either cereal to a child aged four to six? Why or why not?

_____

_____

_____

Nutrition Facts
Serving Size ¾ Cup (30g)
Servings per Container 14

Amount Per Serving	Cereal	With ½ Cup Skim Milk
Calories	120	160
Calories from Fat	25	25

	% Daily Value**	
Total Fat 2.5g*	4%	4%
Saturated Fat 0g	0%	3%
Cholesterol 0mg	0%	1%
Sodium 180mg	8%	10%
Potassium 70mg	2%	8%
Total Carbohydrate 24g	8%	10%
Dietary Fiber 1g	6%	6%
Sugars 12g		
Other Carbohydrate 11g		
Protein 2g		

Vitamin A	25%	30%
Vitamin C	25%	25%
Calcium	4%	15%
Iron	25%	25%
Vitamin D	10%	25%
Thiamin	25%	30%
Riboflavin	25%	35%
Niacin	25%	25%
Vitamin B_6	25%	25%
Folic Acid	25%	25%
Phosphorus	6%	20%
Magnesium	4%	8%
Zinc	2%	6%
Copper	2%	2%

*Amount in cereal. A serving of cereal plus milk provides 0.5g saturated fat, <5mg cholesterol, 240mg sodium, 270mg potassium, 30g carbohydrate (18g sugar) and 6g protein.
**Percent Daily Values are based on a 2,000 calorie diet. Your daily values may be higher or lower depending on your calorie needs:

		Calories	2,000	2,500
Total Fat	Less than		65g	80g
Sat. Fat	Less than		20g	25g
Cholesterol	Less than		300mg	300mg
Sodium	Less than		2,400mg	2,400mg
Potassium			3,500mg	3,500mg
Total Carbohydrate			300mg	375g
Dietary Fiber			25g	30g

Calories per gram: Fat 9 • Carbohydrate 4 • Protein 4

INGREDIENTS: WHOLE OAT FLOUR (INCLUDES THE OAT BRAN), SUGAR, CORN SYRUP, DRIED APPLE PIECES, PARTIALLY HYDROGENATED SOYBEAN OIL, WHEAT STARCH, SALT, CINNAMON, CALCIUM CARBONATE, TRISODIUM PHOSPATE, COLOR AND FRESHNESS PRESERVED BY SODIUM SULFITE, SULFUR DIOXIDE AND BHT.
VITAMINS AND MINERALS: VITAMIN C (SODIUM ASCORBATE), A B VITAMIN (NIACIN), IRON (A MINERAL NUTRIENT), VITAMIN A (PALMITATE), VITAMIN B_6 (PYRI-

Emotional and Social Development from Four to Six

CHAPTER 15

Study Guide

Directions. As you read the chapter, answer the following questions. Later, you can use this guide to study the information in the chapter.

Section 15-1: Emotional Development from Four to Six

1. What major change affects children in this period? _____

_____

2. Briefly describe the general emotional patterns of children from four to six.

   A. Age four: _____

_____

_____

_____

_____

   B. Age five: _____

_____

_____

_____

_____

   C. Age six: _____

_____

_____

_____

_____

3. How does confidence affect initiative? _____

_____

_____

_____

(Continued on next page)

4. Clara Elena became angry at her friend. She started calling the other girl names. Based on average development, how old do you think Clara Elena is? Why?

_____

_____

_____

_____

5. Five-year-old Jesse, starting kindergarten for the first time, is being bothered by a bully at school. If you were Jesse's parent, what would you do?

_____

_____

_____

6. How do children in this period express jealousy? _____

_____

_____

7. What are three ways that children show stress? _____

_____

_____

_____

_____

8. List two advantages and two disadvantages of playing competitively.

Advantages: _____

_____

Disadvantages: _____

_____

Section 15-2: Social and Moral Development from Four to Six

9. Identify the approximate age of the child based on the description given.

A. Erik and his friends rarely quarrel, and they no longer take each other's toys, as they did in the past.

_____

(Continued on next page)

B. Christie wants to spend more time with her friend Alicia than she did last year, but they seem always to be fighting.

_____

C. Maryann took her father by the hand and brought him to the room where she was building with interlocking blocks. "Look at my house!" Maryann said proudly.

_____

D. Kevin and the other boys were playing in the sandbox at preschool, but an argument started when Kevin began to tell the other children how to play.

_____

E. Meg seemed to enjoy playing soccer after school, but after fifteen minutes she drifted out of the game.

_____

F. Cao told Kenny, "You know, Jay still watches baby shows on television," and Kenny laughed.

_____

10. Describe the changes in relationships with family members in these years. _____

_____

_____

_____

11. What change in moral development takes place in this period? How might that affect how parents instruct children these ages?

_____

_____

_____

_____

_____

12. Suppose that you're a parent who sees a broken glass in the kitchen. Five-year-old Kaneesha was the last person to be in the kitchen, as far as you know. You know that children her age may not always tell the truth. What would you do?

_____

_____

_____

(Continued on next page)

Emotional and Social Development from Four to Six   ***Chapter 15 continued***

13. Suppose you work in a child care center and saw a four-year-old hit another child. What would you do?

_____

_____

_____

_____

14. What can parents do to prevent having their children being exposed to violence on television?

_____

_____

_____

_____

Emotional Development from Four to Six

Giving Constructive Criticism

Directions. Children from four to six are generally sensitive to criticism. Unsure of their abilities, they dis-like being told that they did something wrong. Read each of the following statements. In the spaces below each one, write how you would rephrase the statement to make it easier for a child to accept.

1. "You'll never get that tower of blocks to stay up if you don't work more carefully." _____

_____

_____

_____

2. "I don't see any of the things you're describing in that picture. It just looks like a bunch of squiggles to me."

_____

_____

_____

3. "You weren't picked for the team until last because you don't try hard enough." _____

_____

_____

_____

_____

4. "What's wrong with you? Don't you know how to tie your shoes yet?" _____

_____

_____

_____

5. "Go clean your room, and do the whole job this time." _____

_____

_____

_____

Social and Moral Development
from Four to Six

Guiding Children's Behavior

Directions. Two parents who both have five-year-olds met for lunch one day while the children were in school. The following is part of their conversation. Read the dialogue, and then answer the questions that follow.

Lauren:	It's really tough trying to set an example for the kids. Yesterday, we were late for school, and I grabbed Ira's hand and ran across the street just after the light changed. After we got across, Ira said, "You did the wrong thing, Mom. You're supposed to wait until the light changes again!" I told him that there were no cars coming yet, so it was OK, but he shouldn't do that without me.
Andrea:	That's what I tell Doug. "Just do what I say," I tell him, "and you'll be fine. You can do whatever you want when you grow up." Of course, Doug never does what I tell him. You know, I have to tell him all the time to stop interrupting. And he still does it! It drives me crazy.
Lauren:	Ira used to do that, but we came up with a good system. When we're talking, and he wants to say something, he has to raise his hand. When we say something to him, then he can talk. It's just like school—it was very easy for Ira to make it a habit.
Andrea:	That's a great idea! I think I'll try that. Sometimes, though, they're little angels. The other day, I found Doug helping little Addie. He made a shoebox into a crib for her doll. It was so sweet, I almost cried. I told him how nice it was. That made him really happy.

1. What examples of good guidance do the parents mention? _____

_____

_____

_____

_____

2. In which situations would you recommend that the parents act differently? _____

_____

_____

_____

_____

Intellectual Development from Four to Six

Study Guide

Directions. As you read the chapter, answer the following questions. Later, you can use this guide to study the information in the chapter.

Section 16-1: Intelligence and Learning from Four to Six

1. Give an example (different from those in the text) of preoperational thinking among children in this age group in each of the following areas:

A. Use of symbols: _____

B. Make-believe play: _____

C. Egocentric viewpoint: _____

D. Limited focus: _____

2. What does IQ stand for? What does it mean in intelligence testing? _____

_____

_____

_____

_____

3. Why is the value of intelligence tests limited? _____

_____

_____

_____

_____

_____

(Continued on next page)

4. Choosing from the list in the box below, write the letter corresponding to the correct kind of intelligence in the space next to its description.

KINDS OF INTELLIGENCE

A. Verbal-linguistic	**C.** Visual-spatial	**F.** Interpersonal
B. Logical- mathematical	**D.** Musical **E.** Bodily-kinesthetic	**G.** Intrapersonal **H.** Naturalistic

---

_____ Ability to draw or make things

_____ Understanding plants and animals

_____ Communicates well with words

_____ Possessed by athletes and dancers

_____ In touch with own feelings

_____ Ability to get along with others

_____ Ability to find patterns

_____ Linked to rhythm and sounds

5. Why would questions that can be answered "yes" or "no" be less effective in helping children learn?

_____

_____

_____

_____

6. How do rhyming and alphabet books help children learn phonemes? _____

_____

_____

_____

7. What does it mean to be bilingual? _____

_____

_____

8. What kind of books or stories do four- to six-year-olds enjoy? _____

_____

_____

9. What art materials are appropriate for four- to six-year-olds? _____

_____

_____

10. What are finger plays? _____

_____

_____

Section 16-2: The Child in School

11. How does preschool help prepare children for school? _____

_____

_____

_____

12. Why do states require that children have a physical exam and show proof of immunizations before starting school?

_____

_____

_____

_____

13. What tips could you give a parent whose child is about to start kindergarten? _____

_____

_____

_____

_____

14. What changes in language development take place in the years from four to six? _____

_____

_____

15. How can caregivers help a child develop a strong vocabulary? _____

_____

_____

(Continued on next page)

Intellectual Development from Four to Six   *Chapter 16 continued*

16. What four factors are shared by the many definitions of learning disability? _____

_____

_____

_____

_____

_____

17. Describe attention deficit hyperactivity disorder (ADHD) and what causes it? _____

_____

_____

_____

_____

18. What is dyslexia? _____

_____

_____

_____

19. What children are considered to be "gifted children"? _____

_____

_____

_____

20. What problems can gifted and talented children suffer in school? Why? _____

_____

_____

_____

Intelligence and Learning from Four to Six

Deciphering Development

Directions. Use the list of terms from the box below to correctly identify each description or example in the chart below. Write the term in the space provided in the chart. Some terms are used more than once.

TERMS

bilingual	multiple intelligences
dramatic play	phoneme
finger plays	preoperational thinking
intelligence quotient	

Terms	Descriptions or Examples
	A number score that compares how a person performed on a test to others that person's age.
	Sounds that make up words.
	Charney speaks both Korean and English.
	Songs or chants with accompanying hand motions.
	Shown by egocentric viewpoint and limited ability to see other points of view.
	Types include spatial-kinesthetic, musical, and interpersonal.

(Continued on next page)

Intelligence and Learning from Four to Six   *Section 16-1 continued*

Terms	Descriptions or Examples
	Gregg was excited when he got home from school. "Look what I learned today!" he told his father. He stretched out two fingers and put his hand near his head and began to sing, "This is the bunny …"
	Imitating real-life situations, such as playing house or school.
	Period of intellectual development identified by Piaget.
	Average for people of any age is 90 to 110. More intelligent people are said to have scores higher than that average.
	Julie and Kate loved to play store. They filled their "shopping baskets" with plastic fruit and vegetables and then took them to the cash register.
	The children sang "Itsy-Bitsy Spider" and moved their fingers like a spider up the wall.
	Sounds like "oo," "ee," "op," and "ot."
	Able to speak two languages.
	The theory that there are many different ways of using the mind and body to experience the world.
	Can be learned by hearing rhymes and alliteration.

The Child in School

What Is Dyslexia Like?

Directions. In dyslexia, people can read the words on a page, but the brain registers the letters backwards, upside down, or in reversed order. This can make it difficult for the people to read. To understand the problem, try to read the following paragraph. Write what you have read in the space provided.

> Forurg Vieg Prgsibugt Nglsou Roɔʞgrꟈgllrg
> mas ui tdg tdrib prabg mdgu ti mas
> biɔɔovgrbg dg dab byslgaix. Iu dis omu
> mrobg, "I strnpplbs ot nubgrstuba morbg
> tdat ssgwgb ot parlds dgꟈogr uy gygs,
> unwdrss tdat ɔawg ont daɔʞmarbs,
> sgutguɔss tdat mgrg dabr ot prasq.....
> I wabg ti siwqly dy morʞuip darbgr
> aub rgpuol tdau tdg rgst."

_____

_____

_____

_____

_____

_____

_____

_____

The Child from Seven to Twelve

Study Guide

Directions. As you read the chapter, answer the following questions. Later, you can use this guide to study the information in the chapter.

Section 17-1: Physical Growth and Development from Seven to Twelve

1. Describe how children's average height and weight change from ages seven to twelve.

_____

_____

_____

_____

2. What emotional effects can this growth have? Why? _____

_____

_____

_____

3. What is an eating disorder? _____

_____

_____

4. What changes affect boys and girls during puberty?

A. Boys: _____

_____

_____

_____

B. Girls: _____

_____

_____

_____

(Continued on next page)

5. What are the four Dietary Guidelines for a healthy diet? _____

_____

_____

_____

6. Why do some children need to see an orthodontist? _____

_____

_____

7. Mr. Chen is frustrated because he and his teen son seem to argue each night about the son's need to wash before sleeping. What advice would you give Mr. Chen?

_____

_____

_____

_____

8. What causes acne? How can it be treated? _____

_____

_____

_____

Section 17-2: Emotional Development from Seven to Twelve

9. How do children from seven to twelve see their own personalities? _____

_____

_____

_____

_____

10. What are signs of strengthening gender identity? _____

_____

_____

_____

_____

(Continued on next page)

11. Kaleel, in middle childhood, is a happy, outgoing child. Which age do you think he might be? Why?

_____

_____

_____

12. Suki is very absorbed in her own thoughts. She often ignores others, seeming not to care what they say. Is she likely to be in middle childhood or early adolescence? Why?

_____

_____

_____

13. How is anger expressed in children seven to twelve? How long does it last? _____

_____

_____

_____

14. How do children's fears generally change during these ages? _____

_____

_____

_____

15. Why do parents sometimes need to show patience with children in these ages? _____

_____

_____

_____

_____

Section 17-3: Social and Moral Development from Seven to Twelve

16. How do friendships change during the years from seven to twelve? _____

_____

_____

_____

(Continued on next page)

17. Why is the number of friends a child has not a good measure of a child's social health? What is a better way of evaluating that health?

_____

_____

_____

_____

18. What is the difference between peer pressure and conformity? _____

_____

_____

_____

_____

19. Why is teasing so difficult for children in these ages? _____

_____

_____

_____

20. How would you describe the pattern of relationships between children and parents during these years? Why?

_____

_____

_____

_____

21. Why do children these ages have more problems with siblings who are about the same age, rather than those who are much younger or much older?

_____

_____

_____

22. How can parents help children make moral choices when they are not around? _____

_____

_____

_____

(Continued on next page)

Section 17-4: Intellectual Development from Seven to Twelve

23. Characterize the intellectual development of children seven to ten shown in each of the following areas.

   A. Classifying objects: _____

_____

   B. Transitivity: _____

_____

   C. Conservation: _____

_____

24. What is the difference between concrete and formal thinking? _____

_____

_____

_____

25. In what areas do the intellectual abilities of children seven to twelve improve? In what areas do they decline?

   A. Improve: _____

_____

   B. Decline: _____

_____

26. What are some of the benefits of having children these ages attend a middle school? _____

_____

_____

_____

_____

27. What can be done at home to make it easier for children to do homework? _____

_____

_____

_____

THE DEVELOPING CHILD: Student Workbook

Physical Growth and Development
from Seven to Twelve

Examining Physical Growth
and Development

Directions. From ages seven to twelve, children become highly independent. Though they eat, dress, and bathe themselves, they often resist reminders from parents about how and when they should do these things. Sometimes, too, they let fun interfere with meeting these needs. Using the chart below, list three suggestions that children seven to twelve could follow to meet each of those needs in a responsible way.

Need	Suggestions
Bathing	1. _____ 2. _____ 3. _____
Cleaning teeth	1. _____ 2. _____ 3. _____
Handling acne	1. _____ 2. _____ 3. _____
Eating	1. _____ 2. _____ 3. _____

(Continued on next page)

Need	Suggestions
Weight control	1. _____ 2. _____ 3. _____
Dressing	1. _____ 2. _____ 3. _____
Caring for clothing	1. _____ 2. _____ 3. _____
Sleeping	1. _____ 2. _____ 3. _____

THE DEVELOPING CHILD: Student Workbook

Emotional Development from
Seven to Twelve

Identifying Aspects of Personality

Directions. Children from seven to twelve begin to develop a fuller sense of their own personality. That view of themselves contains several elements, including physical appearance, their aptitudes and talents, personal qualities, and social skills—how they get along with others. Read each statement about a young teen below. Identify which aspect of that teen's personality is being described by writing one of the following letters in the answer space: **PA** for physical appearance; **AT** for aptitudes and talents; **PQ** for personal qualities, and **SS** for social skills. Then answer the questions that follow.

_____ **1.** Jay is of average height for his age, but he thinks he's short because his brother is so much taller than him.

_____ **2.** Kelly told her friend, "I'm just a real honest person. I can't stand it when people lie to me."

_____ **3.** "Walt is so easy to get along with," his classmate said. "I always feel comfortable around him."

_____ **4.** Laura practiced playing the piano every day for almost two hours.

_____ **5.** "Amrit is a good worker," his father said approvingly. "He knows how to organize his time and focus on what needs to be done."

_____ **6.** Pete dreaded the first day of school. He hated having to meet new people.

_____ **7.** Tara was tired of the way her hair looked. She wanted to try something new.

_____ **8.** Caridad always saved her math homework for last because it was the easiest subject for her.

_____ **9.** Caleb enjoyed the time he spent at the senior's center. He liked talking to the older people about the lives that they'd led, and he liked seeing how they brightened up when he arrived.

_____ **10.** Every day after school, Marquise made a snack for his younger brother and helped him with his homework until their mother got home from work. "You're my rock," his mother told him. "I know I can count on you."

_____ **11.** Hayley's little sister nestled into her lap, and Hayley read her favorite story to her.

_____ **12.** "Audra is the fastest player on the team," the coach told her father.

_____ **13.** Craig has a hard time controlling his temper.

_____ **14.** Grant shaved his head.

(Continued on next page)

Emotional Development from Seven to Twelve   *Section 17-2 continued*

A. How does your physical appearance contribute to your personality?

_____

_____

_____

B. What are your aptitudes and talents?

_____

_____

_____

C. What personal qualities do you possess?

_____

_____

_____

D. How do you get along with friends? With other family members?

_____

_____

_____

THE DEVELOPING CHILD: Student Workbook

Social and Moral Development
from Seven to Twelve

Handling Peer Pressure

Directions. Described below are several situations in which young teens are facing pressure from friends. In the spaces that follow each description, write down how the teen could resist the pressure to do something he or she didn't want to do.

1. Amie came up to her friend Dominique and said, "I didn't have a chance to finish the homework last night. Let me see yours."

_____

_____

2. While Jared and Alex were looking at the books, Jared whispered to Alex, "Why don't you just take it? They'll never miss it? This store has loads of money."

_____

_____

3. Curtis offered Mary a cigarette. "What's wrong?" he asked when she shook her head, "are you a baby?"

_____

_____

4. "What do you mean you have to be home?" Randall said to Youssef. "It's only nine o'clock. Your parents won't mind if you stay out another hour or so."

_____

_____

5. "That Dierdre is so snooty," Kerri told Robin. "She thinks she's better than everybody. Let's get her into some trouble that she can't talk her way out of!"

_____

_____

Intellectual Development
from Seven to Twelve

SECTION 17-4

Identifying Stages of Intellectual Development

Directions. Read the descriptions of children's intellectual abilities below. Based on what you know about children's intellectual development, indicate whether the child being described is either (A) younger than seven; (B) seven to ten; or (C) twelve or older. Write the letter of the correct response in the space to the left of the description.

_____ 1. Gavin answered the question that included a hypothetical situation.

_____ 2. Nina was able to sort out the large, red marbles from the rest.

_____ 3. Brittany can use abstract thinking to solve problems.

_____ 4. When the water in one glass was poured into a taller, thinner glass, it filled more of the glass. Chuck said that meant there was more water.

_____ 5. When she was called on, Leah answered: "If one-third is more than one-sixth, and one-sixth is more than one-eighth, then one-third is more than one-eighth."

_____ 6. Holly chews on the block to explore it.

_____ 7. Ona is puzzled by the problems she's having at school. She can remember things better, but she just doesn't seem to be able to concentrate as well.

_____ 8. Brook sorted his baseball cards by teams. Then he put the players on each team in alphabetical order.

_____ 9. As Kwana counted, he held up a finger for each number he said.

_____ 10. Shemika said to her friend Danielle, "Suppose the guy who was going out with your best friend asked you out? What would you do then?"

Safety and Health

Study Guide

Directions. As you read the chapter, answer the following questions. Later, you can use this guide to study the information in the chapter.

Section 18-1: Preventing Accidents and Handling Emergencies

1. What can caregivers do to protect infants from each of the following dangers?

A. Falls: _____

_____

B. Choking: _____

_____

C. Poisoning: _____

_____

D. Drowning: _____

_____

2. Compare how infants and toddlers should be placed in automobiles for their safety. _____

_____

_____

_____

_____

3. Children ages one to three can get into danger quickly. Why? What responsibility does that put on caregivers?

_____

_____

4. What three safety measures can be taken to protect children at outdoor play areas? _____

_____

_____

(Continued on next page)

Safety and Health   *Chapter 18 continued*

5. What are the five guidelines for action in an emergency situation? _____

_____

_____

_____

_____

6. What is the phone number "911" used for? Is it used everywhere? _____

_____

_____

7. Why call a poison control center? _____

_____

_____

_____

8. Why is it necessary to catch an animal that bit a person? _____

_____

9. Identify the correct first aid procedure for each of the following:

Problem	Procedure
Animal bites	
Minor cut or scrape	
Nosebleeds	
Bruises	
First-degree burns	
Chemical burns	
Fainting	

(Continued on next page)

THE DEVELOPING CHILD: Student Workbook

Problem	Procedure
Sprained ankle	
Tick bite	
Splinter	

10. How can you tell a first-degree from a second-degree burn? _____

_____

_____

11. What are the signs of choking? Why is it necessary to act quickly? _____

_____

_____

_____

_____

12. What are the signs of shock? _____

_____

_____

13. When are the following rescue techniques used?

A. Artificial respiration: _____

B. CPR: _____

Section 18-2: Preventing Illness and Caring for a Sick Child

14. What are some common signs of illness in children?

A. Infants and toddlers: _____

_____

_____

B. Children five and up: _____

_____

_____

(Continued on next page)

Safety and Health   *Chapter 18 continued*

15. What does "to immunize" mean? What is a vaccine? How do vaccines work? _____

_____

_____

_____

_____

_____

16. What are some examples of diseases that children are immunized against? _____

_____

_____

_____

_____

17. What is an allergy? What effect does it have on the person? _____

_____

_____

_____

18. What is asthma? What can bring on an attack of asthma? _____

_____

_____

_____

19. What is the contagious period of an illness? Why is it necessary to keep a sick child away from other children during this period?

_____

_____

_____

_____

(Continued on next page)

20. Why is it important never to give aspirin to a child with a fever? What medicines could be given for pain relief to a child in this situation?

_____

_____

_____

_____

21. Describe how caregivers can treat sick children at each of the following ages:

A. Infants: _____

_____

B. Ages one to three: _____

_____

C. Ages four and up: _____

_____

22. What are some typical fears children have if they need to be hospitalized? _____

_____

_____

23. How are hospitals trying to help children feel more comfortable? _____

_____

_____

Preventing Accidents and Handling
Emergencies

Taking the Right Steps in an Emergency

Directions. Listed below are several emergency situations. After each situation is a set of steps that should be followed. The steps are in the wrong order, however. Put them in the correct order by writing the numbers from 1 to 5 in the spaces to the left of steps.

1. Florinda enters the kitchen and finds her little brother Manolo lying on the floor unconscious. Next to him is an open bottle of cleanser, knocked over.

_____ Take Manolo to the hospital, as directed.

_____ Look at the label on the bottle to see if the cleanser is poisonous.

_____ Call the poison control center.

_____ Bring the bottle to the phone.

_____ Smell Manolo's breath to see if he swallowed any of the cleanser.

2. Shelly is babysitting five-year-old Matt and three-year-old Chelsea. The children are playing in the backyard. Shelley hears Matt cry out in pain and come running. He says that a bee stung him.

_____ Mix baking soda and water into a paste.

_____ Apply a cold cloth to the area.

_____ Scrape off the stinger.

_____ Watch for signs of an allergic reaction.

_____ Apply the paste to the wound.

3. Chris's nine-month-old sister is eating a snack happily when suddenly he notices that he's not hearing her babbling talk any more. Chris looks over and sees his sister's head leaning to the side of the high chair and is waving her hands in the air.

_____ Use the heel of his hand to give four quick blows between her shoulder blades.

_____ Put two middle fingers below the rib cage and above the navel and thrust up.

_____ Go to his sister and pick her up.

_____ Put her face down over his arm.

_____ Turn her face up.

(Continued on next page)

THE DEVELOPING CHILD: Student Workbook

4. Melissa is out riding her tricycle when she crashes. Sobbing, she shows her father that her knee is scraped and bloody.

_____ Place a clean gauze bandage on the wound and press for several minutes to stop the bleeding.

_____ Cover the wound with an antiseptic ointment.

_____ Wash the area with mild soap and warm water.

_____ Put a clean bandage over the wound.

_____ Pat the area dry with a clean towel.

5. Cindy finds her little son face down in the pool. She takes him out and lays him on the lawn of the backyard.

_____ Turn his head face up and tilt it back slightly so his chin points up.

_____ Listen to learn if her son is breathing.

_____ Take a deep breath.

_____ Put her mouth over the mouth of her son, pinching her son's nostrils shut, and blow air into her son's mouth.

_____ Put her son on his back, turn his head to one side, and try to get rid of any water in his mouth.

Preventing Illness and Caring for a Sick Child

Identifying Childhood Diseases

Directions. Listed below are several common disease symptoms. On the lines below, identify the probable disease, indicate the treatment that should be given to the child, and state whether any medication can be given the child.

1. Symptoms: Runny nose, sneezing, coughing, mild fever, sore throat.

A. Disease: _____

B. Treatment: _____

_____

C. Medication: _____

_____

_____

2. Symptoms: High fever, cough, red eyes followed four days later by blotchy red rash that disappears two days later.

A. Disease: _____

B. Treatment: _____

_____

C. Medication: _____

_____

3. Symptoms: Rash of tiny red pimples; low or no fever.

A. Disease: _____

B. Treatment: _____

_____

C. Medication: _____

_____

(Continued on next page)

4. Symptoms: High fever, chills and shakes, body ache.

   A. Disease: _____

   B. Treatment: _____

   _____

   C. Medication: _____

   _____

5. Symptoms: Headache, fever, sore throat, fine red rash, swollen lymph nodes.

   A. Disease: _____

   B. Treatment: _____

   _____

   C. Medication: _____

   _____

6. Symptoms: High fever, pulling at ears.

   A. Disease: _____

   B. Treatment: _____

   _____

   C. Medication: _____

Special Challenges for Children

Study Guide

Directions. As you read the chapter, answer the following questions. Later, you can use this guide to study the information in the chapter.

Section 19-1: Exceptional Children

1. How can parents' attitudes toward a disabled child affect the child's future? _____

_____

_____

_____

_____

2. How do children with disabilities—and other children—benefit from the policy of inclusion?

_____

_____

_____

_____

3. Why is early detection important for children with disabilities? _____

_____

_____

_____

4. How do children with disabilities gain from learning self-care skills? _____

_____

_____

_____

5. How are children with mental disabilities different from other children? _____

_____

_____

_____

(Continued on next page)

THE DEVELOPING CHILD: Student Workbook

6. How should caregivers present directions to children with mental disabilities so those children will learn how they are expected to behave?

_____

_____

_____

7. What kinds of behaviors might indicate that a child has an emotional disability?

_____

_____

_____

8. What changes in family interactions might a behavioral therapist suggest to help a child with an emotional disturbance?

_____

_____

9. Where can parents of children with disabilities get help and advice? _____

_____

_____

Section 19-2: Child Abuse and Neglect

10. What is child abuse? _____

_____

_____

11. List the four categories of child abuse. _____

_____

_____

_____

12. Why are people who were abused as children more likely to become abusers themselves?

_____

_____

_____

(Continued on next page)

Special Challenges for Children   *Chapter 19 continued*

13. What incorrect beliefs about children do many child abusers possess? _____

_____

_____

_____

_____

14. What should you do if you suspect a child is being abused? _____

_____

_____

15. What is the purpose of crisis nursery? _____

_____

_____

Section 19-3: Family Stresses

16. What are the four guidelines for telling children that the parents will divorce? _____

_____

_____

_____

_____

17. What steps can parents take after a divorce to help the children cope? _____

_____

_____

_____

18. How are children at each of the following ages likely to view death?

   A. Two-year-old: _____

   B. Four-year-old: _____

   C. Six-year-old: _____

   D. Ten-year-old: _____

(Continued on next page)

19. Why is it important to be honest with children when somebody they know dies?

_____

_____

_____

20. What kinds of feelings might a child have if a parent dies? How can the child be helped to cope with those feelings?

_____

_____

_____

21. Why is moving stressful to children? What can families do to make it easier? _____

_____

_____

_____

_____

22. Should children be told of family financial problems? Why or why not? _____

_____

_____

_____

23. What is co-dependency? _____

_____

_____

_____

Special Children

Living with Children with Disabilities

Directions. Suppose you are a professional counselor who has a radio call-in show. People phone you with their problems, and you try to offer them some suggestions for handling those problems. Below are examples of several calls that you have received recently. In the spaces following each caller's comments, write what you would advise.

1. My ten-year-old is mentally disabled. The school system has a new policy now and wants to put him in the regular classroom. I'm very worried that the other children will pick on him and tease him. The kids in the neighborhood are fine with him, but in regular classes, there will be others who don't know him. I don't want his feelings to be hurt. Should I fight this idea?

_____

_____

_____

_____

2. My six-year-old daughter has never done well with other people. She cries whenever she's in a new situation, and it's gotten worse now that she's started school. She hates to go out in the morning. What might be the problem?

_____

_____

_____

_____

3. We've just found out that our baby is deaf. I don't know what to do. How can we communicate with her if we can't talk to her?

_____

_____

_____

_____

Child Abuse and Neglect

Breaking the Cycle of Child Abuse

Directions. Child abuse and neglect involve critical and delicate issues that affect many children. These children will be unable to develop their full potential and become healthy adults unless steps are taken to help them. In the following boxes, write down your ideas about how to break the cycle of child abuse. What can be done in the family, the legal system, and society in general to help in the following four areas?

To Identify Potential Abusers	To Treat Abusers and Potential Abusers

To Prevent Child Abuse	To Treat the Victims

Family Stresses

Thinking About Family Crises

Directions. Divorce, moving, and death can all cause family problems. For each statement about these situations, place next to it the number that expresses your feelings about that statement. For the ratings, choose from the list below. Be prepared to discuss your answers.

```
RATINGS
1 = Strongly disagree      4 = Agree
2 = Disagree               5 = Strongly agree
3 = No opinion
```

Divorce

_____ **1.** It's better for children to live with both parents, even if they often fight, than to suffer through a divorce.

_____ **2.** Children do best if they live with the mother after a divorce.

_____ **3.** If their parents divorce, boys need an adult male they can look up to and talk to.

_____ **4.** After a divorce, children should spend equal time in each parent's home.

_____ **5.** Once parents divorce, neither one should remarry until the children are old enough to have their own homes.

_____ **6.** Divorce is easier for a child to accept if he or she has brothers or sisters.

_____ **7.** Divorce is harder on younger than older children.

_____ **8.** Divorce is usually the fault of one of the partners.

Moving

_____ **9.** Moving doesn't cause problems for children before they start school.

_____ **10.** Moving is easy on a family if they stay within the same town. It's only hard if they go farther away.

_____ **11.** Moving is easier for children if they're at an age when they're going to change schools anyway.

_____ **12.** Children shouldn't think about their friends in the last few weeks before a move because it will only make them sad.

(Continued on next page)

THE DEVELOPING CHILD: Student Workbook **161**

_____ **13.** Moving is painful and sad. There aren't any benefits from a move.

_____ **14.** Getting to know a new place after moving can be fun.

Death

_____ **15.** A parent widowed by the death of a spouse shouldn't remarry.

_____ **16.** After a child's parent dies, the surviving parent and the children shouldn't talk about the parent who died.

_____ **17.** After someone dies, parents should wait until the child is ready to talk and not bring the subject up.

_____ **18.** A quick accidental death is harder for family members to accept than a prolonged illness.

_____ **19.** Children under ten shouldn't attend funerals.

_____ **20.** Parents shouldn't make a big deal of it when a child's pet dies.

Caring for Children

Study Guide

Directions. As you read the chapter, answer the following questions. Later, you can use this guide to study the information in the chapter.

Section 20-1: Providing Short-Term Child Care

1. What details need to be agreed to between a babysitter and a child's parent before a babysitting job can begin?

_____

_____

_____

2. What are the advantages of arriving early for a babysitting job? _____

_____

_____

_____

3. What are three characteristics of a good care provider? _____

_____

_____

4. What are the five most important rules of caring for infants? _____

_____

_____

_____

_____

5. How does caring for toddlers and preschoolers differ from caring for a baby? _____

_____

_____

_____

(Continued on next page)

THE DEVELOPING CHILD: Student Workbook

6. What is authority? How can a babysitter's authority be established? _____

_____

_____

_____

7. Sabrina was babysitting Keith, age six, and Davey, age four. The two boys were wrestling each other. Sabrina told them to stop, but they didn't. A few minutes later, Keith hit his arm against the leg of a chair and began to cry. Sabrina made sure that Keith hadn't suffered a serious injury, then she had to decide what to do. If you were Sabrina, would you punish the children? If so, how? If not, what would you do?

_____

_____

_____

8. What should you do about fire safety when beginning a babysitting job? _____

_____

_____

_____

_____

Section 20-2: Participating in Child Care and Education

9. How can an early childhood classroom be made comfortable for children? How do children benefit from this?

_____

_____

_____

10. What is a learning center? Name one and describe the kinds of materials is might contain.

_____

_____

_____

_____

(Continued on next page)

Caring for Children   *Chapter 20 continued*

11. How can the different learning centers be made separate from one another? _____

_____

_____

_____

12. What is the importance of health care routines? _____

_____

_____

_____

13. What are four basic health rules that children in an early childhood classroom can follow?

_____

_____

_____

_____

_____

_____

14. Why do children benefit from having a variety of activities? _____

_____

_____

_____

15. What do children need to accomplish in making the transition from one activity to another?

_____

_____

_____

16. What information is contained on a planning chart? _____

_____

_____

_____

(Continued on next page)

17. What information is needed on a lesson plan, which details each activity? _____

_____

_____

18. In what four ways can positive behavior be promoted in the classroom? _____

_____

_____

_____

19. How would you explain to children ages three to five the rule "Be a friend to other people"?

_____

_____

_____

20. What would be an appropriate reward for good behavior for children in each of the following groups:

A. Infants: _____

B. Ages one to three: _____

C. Ages four and up: _____

21. What would you do if one four-year-old took away the toy that another four-year-old was playing with?

_____

_____

_____

Providing Short-Term Child Care

Identifying Learning Opportunities

Directions. The chart that follows lists many different toys and objects that can be used as toys. Complete the chart by indicating what ages the toy is appropriate for and what skills or concepts children can learn from those toys.

Toy or Object	Appropriate Age	Skill or Concept Learned
Bean bags		
Empty egg cartons		
Mirrors		
Wooden blocks		
Paper and scissors		
Dress-up clothes		
Crayons		
Drums		
Push-and-pull toys		

(Continued on next page)

THE DEVELOPING CHILD: Student Workbook

Toy or Object	Appropriate Age	Skill or Concept Learned
Play dough		
Mobiles		
String and large beads		
Rattles and squeaky toys		
Socks		
Stacking toys		
Alphabet blocks		
Shape sorter		
Stuffed animals		

Participating in Child Care and Education

Testing Your Safety Ideas

Directions. Read each statement below about safety in the early childhood classroom. If you believe the statement is a good safety rule, place a check mark (✔) in the column "Agree." If you think it is *not* a good safety rule, place the check mark (✔) in the column "Disagree." Be prepared to defend your answers.

Agree   **Disagree**   **Statement**

1. Adults should follow safety rules themselves because young children learn by example.

2. If children are entering or leaving through a door, an adult should stand nearby and close the door after all the children have passed.

3. Children should not be allowed to build wooden block towers higher than their shoulders.

4. Children should all remain seated until they're done eating.

5. Outdoor play equipment can include frisbees and hard balls.

6. A child's hands should be free when climbing or when riding a wheeled toy.

7. Because children enjoy throwing sand, they should be allowed to as long as no one else is nearby.

8. Children should not be allowed to play with toys on ramps, walkways, and steps.

9. Children should not run with objects in their hands.

10. Harmonicas, whistles, and balloons can be shared.

11. Climbing is an important skill, so children should be allowed to climb on fences, tables, and trees.

12. A good way for preschoolers to get rid of their aggression is to run wheeled vehicles into a wall.

13. Sticks or pointed objects are unsafe for play.

14. During quiet periods, children can amuse themselves with pennies, marbles, or paper clips.

15. Running in the building is acceptable as long as few children are present.

(Continued on next page)

Agree	Disagree	Statement
_____	_____	**16.** It is dangerous to have sand, liquid, or small objects on the floor, and they must be removed at once.
_____	_____	**17.** An art smock should be long enough to reach the floor.
_____	_____	**18.** Lifting a child by the hands and arms is dangerous.
_____	_____	**19.** Crayons and markers in the art area should be nontoxic.
_____	_____	**20.** Safety instruction is not possible with preschool children.